WILD
swimming

wild-swimming *(vb.)*:

1. Swimming in natural waters such as rivers, lakes and waterfalls. Often associated with picnics and summer holidays.

2. Dipping or plunging in secret or hidden places, sometimes in wilderness areas. Associated with skinny-dipping or naked swimming, often with romantic connotations.

3. Action of swimming wildly such as jumping or diving from a height, using swings and slides, or riding the current of a river.

Text and photos by
Daniel Start

Wild Swimming

First published in the
United Kingdom in 2008 by

Punk Publishing Ltd
26 York Street, London W1U 6PZ
Copyright © Punk Publishing Ltd 2008

Text and photographs
© Daniel Start 2008

Some additional photographs
credited where used.

A catalogue record of this book is
available from the British Library.

ISBN-13: 978-0-9552036-7-1

10 9 8 7 6 5 4 3 2 1

www.punkpublishing.com

www.wildswimming.com

Contents

Swims by Region

Scotland
and North

Lakes
and Dales

Central
and East

Wales

South

South West

How to find the swims:

Once you have decided which region you are interested in, turn to the swim locator map at the start of that section where you'll find the swims (**1–150**) together with the highlights of the region.

Look out for the corresponding swim box in the subsequent pages for details on water quality, directions, access and much more. Or just turn to any page and dive in for a refreshing and fascinating dip into Britain's idyllic freshwater hideaways.

South West

South

Central and East

Wales

Lakes and Dales

Scotland and North

Beginnings

When I was young, the rambling old house we shared with two other families came with lakes, woods, streams and an overgrown boat house. Situated deep in the heart of the Wye valley, close to the Welsh border, it was here my brother and I first learned to make dams, build rafts and explore the river.

I loved one stream in particular. Gushing and snaking its way down the side of the Black Mountains, its mossy dingles and foxglove-filled dells enchanted me. Plunging into deep pools and sliding down chutes, my brother and I spent much of our summer squealing and slithering along its helter-skelter of cascades.

Twenty years on I could still hear that river as I worked my way through a variety of office jobs. When I told friends about the fun we had, they too recalled favourite swimming memories, glazing over with nostalgic fondness. During one particularly sweltering summer night, I began imagining a journey that would take me back to all these beloved childhood places. And so the idea evolved: with the help of my friends I would compile a connoisseurs' handbook of the most delicious dips and drinkable vistas of Britain – finding the places where people still swim and collecting stories about the art of wild-swimming.

Introduction

One branch of evolutionary theory, expounded by Sir Alistair Hardy in the 1950s, suggests that being by and in water is more than just a pleasure, it is at the core of our human condition. During the ten million years of the Pliocene world droughts, while our species was busy evolving into uprightness, we did not, suggests Hardy, choose the arid deserts of Africa as our home, as mainstream evolutionists believe, but the more tempting turquoise shallows of the nearby Indian Ocean. There we became semi-aquatic coastal waders. Our subsequent life on dry land is a relatively recent and bereft affair.

Could this explain some of our more peculiar habits and features? Apart from the proboscis monkey, we are the only primate that regularly plays in water for the sheer joy of it, and whose offspring take naturally to water from birth. We are also alone in having subcutaneous fat, like a whale's blubber, for buoyancy and warmth. We are almost hairless, like the dolphin, and what little hair remains is arranged to make us streamlined for swimming.

Perhaps this is why Greek art and mythology abounds in stories of water nymphs, naiads and sirens as magical, sexual, mischievous creatures, inhabiting their wild 'nymphaea': natural pools, rivers and swimming holes, so beautiful they lure unwitting mortals to their watery ends.

As the nineteenth century dawned, a new era of contemporary European artists were rediscovering the appeal of the swimming hole. The waterfall, surrounded by trees and mountains, was now regarded as the quintessence of beauty. Wordsworth, Coleridge and de Quincy spent much time bathing in the mountain pools of the Lake District. The study and search for the 'picturesque' and 'sublime' – an almost scientific measure of loveliness and proportion in the landscape – had reached epidemic proportions. The fashionable tours of Provence or Tuscany were replaced by trips to the valleys of Wales, and the dales of Cumbria and Yorkshire, as Turner and Constable painted a prodigious flow of falls, tarns and ponds.

As the Romantic era took hold, the water held its place in the artists' gaze. Ruskin and others moved south to paint the river pools of Cornwall and Devon. Meanwhile, Charles Kingsley was dreaming of water babies on the Devon Dart and Henry Scott Tuke was opening his floating studio in Falmouth, painting scenes of children swimming in the river. Soon Francis Meadow Sutcliffe gained notoriety for his *Water Rats* photograph of naked boys, while across the Atlantic Thomas Eakins was creating a stir with his homoerotic painting of the *Swimming Hole*. Water and nudity were pushing at the boundaries of rigid Victorian society and creating space for new ideas, freedoms and creativity.

Pools and springs have long been revered by our Celtic and pagan ancestors. Even the Romans built shrines to the water goddesses, and several accompany the bathhouses along Hadrian's Wall. Fresh water was seen as a sort of interface with the spirit world, a place where miracles – or curses – could manifest. 'Mermaid Pools' dot our Pennine mountain tops and ancient holy wells and springs are found across the Welsh and Cornish hills. No wonder, then, when Christianity came the Britons were quick to embrace river baptism as a doorway to a new god.

From a secular perspective the health and psychological benefits of dipping in natural waters were also long known. George Bernard Shaw, Benjamin Britten, Charles Darwin and Florence Nightingale were all advocates of regular cold baths to strengthen the mental constitution and physical state. Cold immersion soothes muscle aches, relieves depression and boosts the immune system. All wild-dippers know the natural endorphin high that raises mood, elates the senses and creates

With worries about climate change, obesity and urban youth crime, we need, more than ever, new and exciting ways for our children to engage with the natural world and to explore it in safe and responsible ways. Swimming is the favourite sporting activity for girls and is second only to football for boys. Perhaps opening up our rivers, lakes and waterfalls again can provide new opportunities to satisfy an appetite for adventure while attaching new meaning to the environment and the wild.

an addictive urge to dive back in. However the world seemed before a swim, it looks fantastic afterwards.

The long-term impacts are also well researched: NASA studies have shown that, over a 12-week period, repeated cold swimming leads to substantial bodily changes known as 'cold adaptation'. These bring down blood pressure and cholesterol, reduce fat disposition, inhibit blood clotting and increase fertility and libido in both men and women. Far from quelling passion, a cold shower will boost vitality and desire.

By the 1870s, river- and lake-based recreation was entering mainstream culture. London was expanding at a rate of knots and the middle- and working-class population woke up to the potential of the Thames, with its villages, boats and watering holes lying only a cheap rail fare away.

'We would have the river almost to ourselves,' recalled Jerome K. Jerome, 'and sometimes would fix up a trip of three or four days or a week, doing the thing in style and camping out.' In 1888 he wrote the best-selling *Three Men in a Boat*, which was a manifesto for a simple way of living: close to nature, with river swimming before breakfast. Ratty declared in *Wind in the Willows* that there 'was nothing, simply nothing, more worthwhile than messing about in boats' and by 1909 Rupert Brooke was writing poems about bathing in Grantchester.

It was an idyllic period. Europe had been relatively peaceful for a hundred years. It was an age of relaxed elegance, of 25-mile-a-day walking tours, sleeping under canvas and bathing in the river. Brooke spent his days studying literature, swimming, living off fruit and honey and commuting to Cambridge by canoe. His passion for the outdoor life was shared by writers Virginia Woolf and E. M. Forster, philosophers Russell and Wittgenstein, economist Keynes and artist Augustus John. As they swam naked at Byron's Pool in moonlight and practised their 'belly-floppers' in picnic diving practice along the Cam this nucleus formed the emerging Bloomsbury Group and what Woolf later dubbed the 'Neo-Pagans'.

Grantchester Meadows became the site of one of the first formal bathing clubs in the country, with an elegant pavilion, separate changing areas and stone steps down into the warm waters of the river Cam. Similar clubs, 'Parsons' Pleasure' and later 'Dames' Delight', quickly followed at the Cherwell in Oxford. Soon every major public school was following suit with its own special riverside swimming facilities. By 1923 over 600 informal river swimming clubs were in existence around the country with regular inter-county river swimming competitions and galas. Henry Williamson was swimming with *Tarka the Otter*, and Arthur Ransome immortalised the Lake District in *Swallows and Amazons*. Wild-swimming had reached its heyday.

The post-war years brought a great thrust of industry and development and rivers bore the brunt of the pollution. By the 1960s pesticides had driven the West Country population of otters to near extinction. It was not until new legislation was introduced in the 1970s and 1980s that the trend began to turn. Thirty years on, over 70 per cent of our rivers are in good or excellent condition again. They are hidden havens for wildlife once more, secret corridors into forgotten corners of our countryside.

For many of us this kind of communion with our ecology is moving. It's a place to seek inspiration, intuition and peace and also to be humbled by the immensity and wonder of nature. These are places where children see their first kingfisher or find their first otter track. Here we learn to play Pooh sticks and build dams before falling asleep in the grass. Use this book to open up a fresh world of adventures, romantic escapades and family days out. The water's fresh, so pick up, strip off and jump in!

'I can go right up to a frog in the water and it will show more curiosity than fear. The damselflies and dragonflies that crowd the surface of the moat pointedly ignore me, just taking off for a moment to allow me to go by them, then landing again on my wake. In the water you are hidden and submerged, enveloped in the silkiness of a liquid that is the medium of all life on earth.'

The late Roger Deakin, author of *Waterlog*, naturalist and forefather of wild-swimming, describing swimming in his moat in Suffolk.

Getting Started

A scorching hot summer's day is a great time for swimming, and it can be exciting on rainy or cooler days too. The key is to arrive at the swimming hole so hot and sweaty you can't wait to strip off and plunge in.

10 ways to be wild and safe

1 Never swim in canals, urban rivers, stagnant lakes or reedy shallows

2 Keep cuts and wounds covered with waterproof plasters

3 Never swim in flood water and be cautious of water quality during droughts

4 Avoid contact with blue–green algae scum

5 Never swim alone and keep a constant watch on weak swimmers

6 Never jump into water you have not thoroughly checked for depth and obstructions

7 Always make sure you know how you will get out before you get in

8 Don't get too cold – warm up with exercise and warm clothes before and after a swim

9 Wear footwear if you can

10 Ask local fishermen if you are concerned about a local pollution problem

Turn to pages 252–253 for more detailed information

Staying warm: Plan a good hearty walk to get there, and put on lots of warm clothes before you arrive. Once you're in the water it takes a few minutes before the cold feeling goes away, so persevere. In general, the more you swim in cold water the less you feel the cold and the greater the health benefits of what is called 'cold adaptation'. Don't stay in too long without a wetsuit, though, and definitely get out and warm up after 20 minutes or if you start to shiver. Put on warm clothes immediately after a swim and combine this with something active: walk up a hill or do some star jumps. There are ideas for warming games at the back of the book as well as instructions on building a sauna!

Equipment: You'll have more confidence, and be better able to explore, if you have footwear (e.g. old trainers, jelly beans etc) and goggles. A normal surfing wetsuit, a sleeveless wetsuit top or a specialist triathlon wetsuit will all help you stay warm longer. Make sure you bring towels, a picnic rug, midge repellent, suntan lotion, sunhats and plastic bags for all your wet kit. Inflatables are popular but make sure people won't drift away on them, especially non-swimmers. A proper buoyancy aid (about £40) is safer, and fun too.

Skinny-dipping: If you come across a magical pool on a walk it's quite possible to swim even without any kit. Wear your undies or go naked if it is secluded. If you have no towel wipe most of the water off with your hands then sacrifice one item of clothing to dry yourself with or travel with a small, light cotton sarong.

Water quality: All swims in this book are good quality and graded A to C, equivalent to the Environment Agency's ratings: 'very good', 'good' and 'fairly good'. See page 254 for more detailed information.

Finding the swimming holes in this book

Using online maps: Every one of the 150 swims has been located with both a postcode (useful for those relying on satnav devices), and a UK Ordnance Survey (OS) grid reference of two letters and six numbers. The postcode only pinpoints the swim to within about 1km (in rural areas), so a distance is sometimes given next to it e.g. '500m N' means 'look 500m north of the postcode'. OS grid references are more accurate, down to 100m, and can be used in www.multimap.com which provides free 1:50,000 OS mapping (the purple Landranger maps) essential for navigation in the countryside. Hover over the 'map' button and the OS map option

appears, but only at certain zoom levels. You can only find the 1:25,000 OS mapping (the orange Explorer maps), even better for finding remote places, at www.ordnancesurvey.co.uk/getamap. Click on the magenta 'Get-a-Map' button and type in your grid reference with no spaces. Both sites allow you to print. Remember when using a grid reference the third number tells you how many hundred metres east of the last grid line you are, and the last number tells you how many hundred north. All the links to the maps you need, plus links to 3D aerial photography, overviews and ideas for new places to visit can be found at **www.wildswimming.com**

Using the directions: You can also rely on the written directions alone. The abbreviations are the points of the compass: N, NE, E, SE, S, SW, W and NW. Left (L) and right (R) are always the river's L and R, i.e. facing in the direction of river flow. Directions are always given from the 'swim town' unless indicated. Sometimes you will need to measure distances in your car, in kilometres, or walking, in 100m. If you need to convert, 1km = 0.6 miles and 1m = 1.1 yard. Walking 1km takes about 20 minutes on flat ground. The additional swims in each box have less detailed directions but always have a grid reference for use with the online maps.

Swims at a Glance

Great for Paddling

Mainly shallow and popular with families

Literary Swims

Where famous poets, writers or artists once swam

Skinny-dipping

Remote and secluded, perfect for a natural dip

Perfect Picnics

**Beautiful places, not far from car parking
and with good picnic areas or grassy banks**

Leave the Car at Home

Within 20 minutes walk of a train station

Go Cycling

On dedicated cycle trails or routes

Canoeing and Boating

Great for canoeing. At some (marked with an *) you can hire a canoe or rowboat

Pubs

A cosy pub with great food just a splash away

Camping

Fantastic river or lakeside camping. Good for a moonlight swim perhaps?

Jumping

Famous for having deep water into which you can jump from a bridge or ledge. See page 252 for safety advice

Tubing and Water Fun

Great for playing in surf or current, or using a rubber ring

Waterfalls and Plunge Pools

Magically situated under waterfalls, big and small

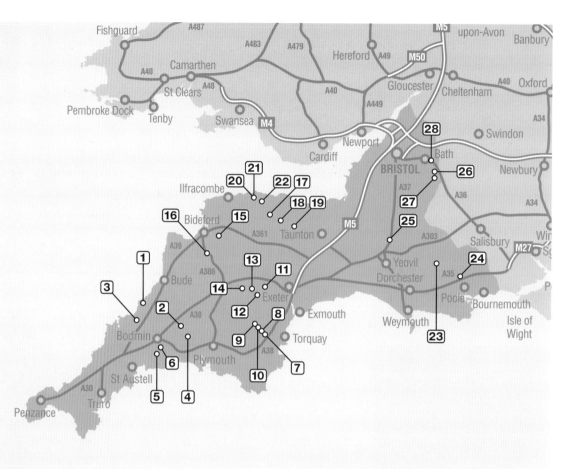

Highlights

1 King Arthur's knights were baptised in this mystical waterfall before beginning their quest for the Holy Grail

2 Some say the Beast of Bodmin still roams these wild and legend-filled moors

3 Camp in the tipi village by this swimming lake set in a magical reclaimed quarry

4–6 Shaded, dappled pools are the headwaters of the beautiful River Fowey at Cornwall's Golitha Falls

8–10 Close to the birthplace of Charles Kingsley these remote river pools on the Dart are surrounded by steep lush forest and inspired the tale of *The Waterbabies*

11 Plunge pools cascade one into the other in these Victorian man-made jacuzzis on the River Teign beneath Castle Drogo

13–14 Dartmoor used to be a volcanic island that erupted out of a shallow tropical sea. These mountain pools provide stunning views from on high

15–16 Swim with *Tarka the Otter* in the rivers that inspired Henry Williamson's famous novel

19 Paddle, swim and eat a pub lunch at this popular and ancient 'Clapper Bridge' made of great obelisk-sized stones

20–21 Play in wooded pools and waterfalls in the gorge above Watersmeet near Lynmouth

22 Camping, horse-riding, paddling and plunging along the valley that inspired the tale of *Lorna Doone*

23 Swim along the famous Dorset Stour where Thomas Hardy spent the happiest years of his life

25 A traditional and very English ecclesiastical swim alongside the church at West Lydford in Somerset

26 Picnic by the river and exchange favourite wild-swimming locations at Britain's longest established river swimming club

28 Swim and play at one of the longest river weirs in the country

SouthWest

The high moors of Bodmin, Dartmoor and Exmoor dominate this region providing the headwaters for fantastic swimming in the Fowey, Dart and Barle and the Tarka region of the Torridge and Taw. Heading east into the gentle landscape of Somerset and Dorset you'll find riverside churches, outdoor swimming clubs and the prettiest of weir-pools.

△ **1** St Nectan's Kieve plunge pool, Tintagel

North Cornwall and Bodmin

Treading gingerly down the wet slate steps I descended into the veil of mist that rises from St Nectan's Kieve. Found in a hidden valley only a few miles from the Arthurian castle of Tintagel, deep in the shadow of the gorge, this 'kieve' – or basin – is part of an extraordinary double waterfall which for centuries was used for baptisms.

St Nectan, the hermit who lived here in the hermitage around 480AD, was one of the holiest of Cornish saints. It's easy to see why this place was revered. The flow of the water has sculpted a deep cylindrical well and a perfect man-sized hole through which the water spills. This upper pool is out of reach, but the lower pool is deep enough for an exhilarating splash and plunge.

The guardians of this site, who run the tiny tea shop above, don't mind bathing as long as it is done with sincerity and respect. This has long been a place of pilgrimage and immersion and it was here that King Arthur's knights were baptised before they set out on their quest to recover the Holy Grail. Today small shrines of cairns and photographs of loved ones have been set up on the surrounding rocky ledges. Little light filters down here, but hundreds of coloured ribbons tied to branches and rocks give the cavern a fluttering glow, like a pagan May Day.

△ 3

△ 2

Those interested in Arthurian legends should also visit Dozmary Pool, where the ghostly hand reputedly appeared to take the sword Excalibur when the knight Sir Bedivere returned it to the lake. Whirlpools are said to rage here to this day. On top of Bodmin moor on a sunny August day, clouds racing across the sky, Dozmary seems rather benign and the swimming a little shallow. The shores of Colliford lie across the field and provide a more satisfying swim. This is Cornwall's largest and highest lake. It is also situated close to the famous Jamaica Inn, setting for Daphne du Maurier's evocative novel of smugglers and pirates.

If you're looking for somewhere to stay then consider splashing out on a few nights in a romantic tipi by a turquoise quarry lake down near Port Isaac. The land has been in the same family for generations but when the quarry went out of business forty years ago the owner, Lizzie, decided to let it go wild, creating a network of forest clearings with tipis all around the lake. Now families come and stay throughout the summer.

'In the midst of the wild moors, far from any dwelling, there lieth a great standing water called Dosmery Pool. The country people said… that it did ebb and flow, that it had a whirlpool in the midst thereof, and that a faggot once thrown there into was taken up at Foy haven, six miles distant.' from Richard Carew's *Survey of Cornwall*, 1602

Leaving my clothes in a heap I dived in to join the melée, the late afternoon light shining through the leaves. The underwater zone felt white, opaque and was flavoured with minerals. Almost before I had surfaced someone dive-bombed me from a tree and I raced for control of an abandoned Lilo. At the far end of the quarry a willowy boy stood alert at the prow of his canoe searching for trout below.

Later that evening we prepared a small fire and I retired to my tipi at the edge of one of the clearings. Towels were being hung out on the guy ropes to dry, swimming costumes adorned the totem poles and I could still hear the sound of splashing from the lake. This is a little lost world of canoes, swimming and Hiawathas.

North Cornwall and Bodmin

1 St Nectan's Kieve

Town: Tintagel, 2km
Grid ref: SX 081885
Postcode: PL34 0BE (1km SE)

Water quality: A
Depth/size: paddle, plunge

Walking: 20 mins, moderate
Train: Bodmin Parkway, 17km
Extras: Teashop and chapel

ⓘ A tall, slender waterfall at the head of a wild woody dingle. It falls into a high basin, flows through a circular hole and drops into a small plunge pool, 1.5m deep, 5m across. Prayer flags and shrine room. Small tea room in hermitage above. Many steps. Entrance £3.

▶ Follow B3263 2km NE, dir Boscastle. After 2km look out for free waterfall car park on left as you climb hill at entrance to village of Trethevey. Cross road, up track, past St Piran's church on L. Follow signs through fields, then glen, 1km. Up steps to the hermitage and entrance. Open Easter to end October only. Tel. 01840 770760.

2 Colliford Lake and Dozmary

Town: Bolventor, 4km
Grid ref: SX 164721
Postcode: PL14 6PZ (1km S)

Water quality: A
Depth/size: paddle, swim

Walking: 1 min, easy
Train: Bodmin Parkway, 15km
Extras: Visitor and adventure centre

ⓘ A huge moorland lake, the highest and largest in Cornwall. Open access on the west side with chalky, shelving beaches. Dippers, wagtails and sand martins. No trees.

▶ From Bolventor/Jamaica Inn take A30 W, dir Bodmin. After 2km exit for lake. 600m L is the 'Lake Park' café and adventure centre (www.collifordlakepark. com) but no swimming. 1km further on L is car park, lake access and toilet. For more privacy find parking a further 1km on L. Dozmary Pool (SX 193746) is scenic but shallow, 2km S of Bolventor on minor road (dir St Neots) on L.

3 Cornish Tipi Holidays

Town: Port Isaac, 6km
Grid ref: SX 036793
Postcode: PL30 3LW (600m S)

Water quality: A
Depth/size: swim, dive

Walking: 5 mins, easy
Train: Bodmin Parkway, 18km
Extras: Tipis to stay in

ⓘ A luscious, chalk-green, spring-fed quarry lake on private land, part of Cornish Tipi Holidays. Wooded cliffs and banks. Very deep and 200m long. Canoes, islands, fishing, landing bay. You need to be staying to swim: tipis from £275 for a mini break.

▶ Follow narrow coast lane through Port Gaverne, 4km east. Cross B3314 and follow lane 2km. Entrance down narrow track to right (www.cornishtipiholidays. co.uk, 01208 880781) Try also Delford Bridge on the river De Lank 10km to E via lanes. Sandy shallows. On minor lane between Churchtown and Blisland (not via St Breward) PL30 4NL; (SX 115759).

▲ **5** River Fowey at Lanhydrock Estate

South Cornwall and the Fowey

The River Fowey drops in cascades down through dense, sessile oak woodland on the edge of Bodmin moor. There are humid aromatic glens and the trees are draped with rare ferns, mosses and ivy. This area, known as Golitha Falls, is home to otters, which live among the river roots, and bats, which sleep in the old mine workings.

In 1995 a big cat skull was found in the woods and claimed as the final proof of the 'Beast of Bodmin', thought to be a species of small wild cat similar to a puma. The skull in question turned out to be that of a leopard taken from an exotic carpet and planted by a hoaxer.

Where the main path ends, at the beginning of a series of shallow falls, pick your way further down one of the narrow trails. Wagtails criss-cross the stream and a small, gladed pool opens up a few hundred yards below, out of sight of any crowds. When I was there the yellow sand of the stream threw up a golden light on the rocks around as I eased myself into the pool. It was hot and I was tired but the babbling moorland water soon cut through the sweat and grime. It wasn't large or particularly deep, but the stream picked me up and I found a part of the current which, with some careful balancing, held me in position as I swam. Then I flipped on my back and let the flow carry me down into the shallow rapids and ground me in the sand, the water rushing over my shoulders and shins like a spa.

△ **4** Orange Asphodels

△ **6**

△ **4**

After a little doze in the dappled light of the rocky ledges I found a wooded weir pool about another mile or so downstream and camped there discreetly. As dusk gathered around me I sipped whisky and kept a silent vigil for bats and owls. As the evening drew late I thought I saw the luminescent blurs of will-o'-the-wisp in the shadows of the wood before I fell asleep under the trees, looking up at the pale midsummer night sky, with total darkness never quite descending.

Waking early I had a quick splash in the water in bright sunshine before trekking back to the car. I was heading ten miles downstream for the National Trust estate of Lanhydrock House. Once an Augustinian Priory, and the lowest crossing point of the Fowey, it was rebuilt as a great mansion by a Victorian industrialist and is now one of the Trust's most visited properties. The gardens are filled with magnificent magnolia and camellia and the estate stretches for many miles along the Fowey.

Downstream from Respryn Bridge there are bankside deckings which make a good place to change and swim. The water is fast-flowing and refreshing, about five feet deep in places and completely clear. I practised some shallow diving and then swam along the bank, searching for otter holes and examining the oak roots that grow down into the water.

As the morning drew on the path became busy with dog walkers and families playing Pooh sticks so I got dressed and headed upstream to Bodmin Parkway railway station. This was the terminus of the first steam railway in Cornwall, built to bring lime-rich sea sand from Wadebridge for use as fertiliser. A discreet white gate in the corner of the station car park leads down to the old Lanhydrock estate driveway. A wooded stretch of riverbank near here is home to a dark but magical stretch of the river, completely overshadowed by trees and foliage. I swam and floated several hundred yards downstream and then had to tiptoe back barefoot through the undergrowth and creepers to find my pile of clothes. Here, only a mile from the mainline and the 08.35 to Exeter, you can pretend you're lost in a tropical jungle.

South Cornwall and the Fowey

4 Golitha Falls

Town: Liskeard, 8km
Grid ref: SX 223687
Postcode: PL14 6RX (500m S)

Water quality: A
Depth/size: plunge, current

Walking: 20 mins, moderate
Train: Liskeard, 7km
Extras: Trethery Quoit

ⓘ Beautiful stream of young river Fowey runs through ancient oak woodland. First 700m wide path provides access to shallows for paddling. At top of cascades rough tracks continue 200m down to shady secret plunge pool at bottom. Swim against the current. Golden sandy bottom. Don't slip on rocks! Car park and toilet.

▶ On A38 travel west from Liskeard, dir Bodmin. After 3km in Dobwalls, turn R, dir St Cleer. After 3.8km turn L. Car park 400m on L (www.naturalengland.org.uk). Trethery Quoit (King Authur's Quoit) is the most impressive stone burial chamber in Cornwall and can be found at Tremar, 3km E of Golitha.

5 Respryn Bridge

Town: Bodmin, 5km
Grid ref: SX 098634
Postcode: PL30 4AH (200m E)

Water quality: A
Depth/size: paddle, swim

Walking: 10 mins, easy
Train: Bodmin Parkway, 2km
Extras: Lanhydrock House, NT

ⓘ Wooded National Trust estate riverside walk. Some sections 1.5–2m deep. Swim against the current. Wooden bankside deckings (for fishing). Beachy shingle area by footbridge. Popular at weekends.

▶ Follow NT Lanhydrock signposts from either A30 or A38, or take the B3268 off the A390 at Lostwithiel. Don't enter Lanhydrock House main car park but continue on lane 1.5km down to river car park at Respryn Bridge. Cross bridge and walk downstream 150m to fishing platforms, below which are some deepish pools. Continue further 350m to fields on L just before footbridge to find open beachy area.

6 Bodmin Parkway

Town: Bodmin, 5km
Grid ref: SX 107641
Postcode: PL30 4BB (200m W)

Water quality: A
Depth/size: paddle, swim

Walking: 10 mins, easy
Train: Bodmin Parkway, 300m
Extras: Station café, bike route

ⓘ Still in the Lanhydrock Estate, this swim is off the original driveway to the main house from behind the station. Very woody and secluded, like a tropical jungle. Shallow rapids on inside bend, deep on outer bank for a plunge and swim against the current.

▶ From Bodmin Parkway station car park go through white gate, down ramp and underneath railway (follow cycle route signs). 200m after bridge turn R and follow path to pond. Keep to R of pond and cut through the undergrowth to find riverbank hidden behind undergrowth. You can swim here or follow this up to find more jungly pools.

△ **8** Holne Pools, River Dart

South Dartmoor and the Dart

River pools and sandy bays, oak gorges and towering tors. The River Dart is the setting for Charles Kingsley's *The Waterbabies* and one of the most beautiful wild-swimming rivers in the UK.

In a deep gorge far upstream of Newbridge, lying on the flat hot rocks by a gurgling river, I am miles from anywhere. Dense woodland tumbles down the side of the moor, a light spray lifts off the water and the forest twitters with birdsong.

Somewhere along here the hero of *The Waterbabies*, Tom the chimney sweep, was lulled into the water by the fairies. Wrongly accused of theft he escaped across Lewthwaite moor before falling into a deep, exhausted sleep by the river. In his new life underwater he goes in search of the other waterbabies and meets many river creatures on the way: the foolish trout, the wise old salmon, the crafty otter and the trumpeting, happy gnats. He learns many things from them before eventually finding the girl he truly loves.

In the pub in the village of Holne, birthplace of Charles Kingsley, you get the sense they're a little bored of the story but they know the good swimming holes if you ask nicely. Holne Pool is ten minutes' walk down through the fields. You'll find a large rock by a small waterfall, partly in sunshine, partly in shade, a place made for lazy picnics and sunny afternoons.

△ **7**

△ **8** Dartmoor Ponies

Exploring further downstream brings you first to Horseshoe Falls and then Salters Pool and within twenty minutes you'll arrive at the car park of Newbridge where a narrow medieval bridge crosses the river. There's a National Park visitors' hut and an easy walk downstream to the green lawns of Spitchwick Common. With its easy access, gentle pools and good swimming it's popular among families and can be busy on a summer day.

Head back up the other side of the river for a good half an hour and you'll arrive at Wellsfoot Island. On the far side of this romantic piece of woodland there's a red sandy beach in a bend of the river under Holne cliff. This is a fabulous deep pool by a coppice of spindly birch. Feel the fine-grain sand running with the current between your toes.

But the best pools are also the most remote, miles upstream of Newbridge, in the forest halfway to Dartmeet, below Mel Tor. These legendary swimming holes are surrounded by large flat rocks with chutes between them for floating down on rubber rings. Whether you walk up the river from Holne, down from Dartmeet, or you scramble over the steep slopes from Mel Tor, it's quite a trek. You should be able to find your own pool – there are plenty to choose from.

While I mused I suddenly saw three wet-suited swimmers on rings riding the river current who must have come from Dartmeet, at least two miles upstream. 'Is there anywhere good to swim up there?' I called out, ever searching for the perfect pool. 'Everywhere's good to swim!' they replied. Apparently the Dartmeet to Newbridge run is popular with the most daring local swimmers but not generally recommended unless water levels are very low and you know where the waterfalls are. The sport of 'hydrosurfing' is catching on in France, where they gear you up with helmets and padded suits. One local told me that the best swimmers here do it without anything at all, just in their trunks, and have learnt to curl their bodies like eels to pass in between the rocks and slip unharmed over the waterfalls. They can feel the micro-currents with their skin and move through the water like otters. If you're looking for the Dartmoor waterbabies, all grown up, I think these might be them.

South Dartmoor and the Dart

7 Spitchwick Common

Town: Ashburton A38, 5km
Grid ref: SX 715712
Postcode: TQ13 7NT

Water quality: A
Depth/size: paddle, swim, dive

Walking: 5 mins, easy
Train: Totnes, 13km
Extras: Huccaby Farm campsite

ⓘ Peaty water, clean from the mountain, this is the most popular and accessible Dart swimming location, especially in summer. Also known as Deeper Marsh, it has been a bathing place for generations. Grassy flats lead to rocky river shore, deeper on far side with high cliff behind.

▶ From Ashburton A38 follow signs to River Dart Country Park, 2km. Over first medieval bridge, then on to second (Newbridge) with car park and National Park office. Cross road and follow path downstream 300m to Common. Further deepish sections for 300m downstream.

8 Holne Pool

Town: Holne, 0.5km
Grid ref: SX 710702 **PC:** TQ13 7RS
Walking: 15 mins, moderate

ⓘ Small waterfall with sunbathing rock and large pool in secluded Holne Woods, close to Holne and its pub.

▶ As for Spitchwick but turn L, signed Holne, after Country Park. After 1.5km, turning to L goes down into village but 20m on R is footpath down through fields to river. Follow for 500m and 50m after entering woods see river to L. For warming food: www.church-house-inn.co.uk, 01364 631208 in Holne.

9 Mel Tor Pools

Town: Holne, 3.5km
Grid ref: SX 697717 **PC:** TQ13 7RS
Walking: 60 mins, difficult

▶ As for Holne Pool but continue upstream to Sharrah Pool (SX 697717) 2.2km, Mel Pool (SX 697717) 2.9km and Blackpool (SX 685720) 4km. Or access from Mel Tor, or Venford Reservoir.

10 Wellsfoot Island

Town: Ashburton, 5km
Grid ref: SX 705702
Postcode: TQ13 7NX (600m S)

Water quality: A
Depth/size: paddle, swim, dive

Walking: 20 mins, moderate
Train: Totnes, 14km

ⓘ Wonderful wooded island with red sand beach shelving into deep river bend with Holne cliff towering up behind. Rusty, peaty water. Velvet sand. Deep water under cliff. Access only feasible from river's L bank.

▶ From Newbridge car park (see Spitchwick) head upstream on river's L bank (i.e. on car park side). Path is separated from river for three fields but then rejoins it. About 800m/15 mins from car park you'll enter woody common land and see small bridge over stream on L, signed 'private'. The bridge may be private but the island is open access. Beach is on the far side, 50m.

△ **11** Salmon Leaps, Teign

East Dartmoor and the Teign

The most spectacular pools on the Dartmoor Teign are the Victorian 'Salmon Leaps' in woods beneath Castle Drogo. Three rectangular square pools cascade, one into the other, like stacked glasses of champagne.

Castle Drogo was the last castle built in England. Constructed in the 1920s by merchant millionaire Julius Drewe – self-styled as Baron Drogo de Teign – it stands high over the wooded gorge of the Teign. As part of his landscaping project the 'Baron' installed several weirs to create river pools to help stock the river with salmon. The first pool is a long, peaceful stretch of river which runs beneath an elegant suspension bridge. Drewe had a problem because the dam that creates the pool also stopped the upward migration of spawning salmon so to solve this he built an impressive series of salmon 'leaps'.

While the peaceful pool above is popular with the local girls, the salmon leaps are popular with the lads. Each pool is about four feet deep, with a flat concrete bottom. The turbulence literally lifts you off your feet but you soon get the knack of bobbing about in these mountain jacuzzis. The water bubbles wildly as it tumbles from one pool to the other, massaging and pummelling all the muscles in your body.

This river stretch has plenty of Dartmoor legend. A pile of stones up above in the woods is called the Pixie Parlour, after a struggle between a farmhand and a creature from the underworld. There is also a rocking 'logan' stone in the riverbed downstream of the leaps thought to belong to the druids.

△ **13**

△ **13** Rowan at Shilley Pool

△ **11**

Another mile or so downstream you'll find a second weir and river pool before arriving at Fingle Bridge and its pub. This narrow, medieval packhorse bridge was built to service the gorge's once busy industries: corn milling, charcoal burning and bark ripping. It has long been a local beauty, paddling and picnicking spot and even in 1894 the unknown author of *A Gentleman's Walking Tour of Dartmoor*, suggests it is a 'great place for Pic-Nics. We were there in July and found two Pic-Nics going on at once to the tune of a hideous German band'.

Little has changed and if you want more peace and quiet the weir behind Chagford is charming. Or why not visit the town-run swimming pool? It's fed by the river, which comes straight off the moor, though the health-and-safety people still insist that chlorine is added. It was dug in 1947 as a co-operative effort by the village and some of the original old boys still come down to make tea. These days it has solar heaters and an indoor cafe, in case it rains.

An important source of the Teign is Blackaton Brook, which rises by the windswept stone circle of Little Hound Tor, back up on the moor. From here it gathers momentum through Raybarrow Hill and Throwleigh Common before arriving at the tiny and rather secret Shilley Pool. In this sheltered and sunny glen bathers and nymphs have built up a low dam to create a perfect bath.

The water flows in across wide stone slabs, perfect for sunbathing, and the depth reaches about three feet. Lying in the stream, the current scooping eddies along one's length, in the warmth of the afternoon sun, you feel a very small part of some much larger, more wonderful thing. Dartmoor has many secret bathing spots, often difficult to find, and this is one of its most special. Bathe here and you drink in an elixir of all of Dartmoor's magic brew.

East Dartmoor and the Teign

11 Salmon Leaps, Teign

Town: Whiddon Down A30, 3km
Grid ref: SX 723897
Postcode: TQ13 8JN (1km E)

Water quality: A
Depth/size: plunge, swim

Walking: 20 mins, moderate
Train: Exeter, 20km
Extras: Drogo Castle and Fingle Bridge

ⓘ Long river pool in woods beneath Castle Drogo. About 1.5m deep. Weir and footbridge. The Teign cascades into three Victorian square stone plunge pools, each about 1m deep and smooth lined. Great for a pummelling massage!

▶ From A30, Whiddon Down exit, head 4km south on A382. Downhill past pub at Sandy Park and park on road by river bridge. Follow river 1km downstream through fields, then enter woods and find footbridge, pool and salmon leaps. Also paddle near Drewsteighton at Fingle Bridge (SX 743899) www.finglebridgeinn. co.uk, 01647 281287, and weir pool 400m upstream from it.

12 Chagford Lido, Teign

Town: Whiddon Down A30, 5km
Grid ref: SX 707885
Postcode: TQ13 8DA (500m NE)

Water quality: A
Depth/size: plunge, swim, dive

Walking: 1 min, easy
Train: Exeter, 25km
Extras: Tiny historic town of Chagford

ⓘ River-fed swimming pool with café set in fields on outskirts of tiny Chagford. Largest outdoor pool in Devon. Upstream you can swim at shady weir pool behind town.

▶ From Whiddon Down exit of A30 head 4km south on A382, then turn R at Sandy Park by pub. Swimming pool is 1.5km down lane on L, open May– October £1.80 (www.roundash.com/pool. htm). Or go to the pool's source Chagford Weir (SX 700882), 200m further down lane, footpath on R. Cross field to gate on R, then bear L along footpath. Weir pool 500m upstream, along millstream. Shady and steep banks.

13 Shilley Pool

Town: South Zeal, 2km
Grid ref: SX 653912
Postcode: EX20 2QD (600m SW)

Water quality: A+
Depth/size: plunge, shallows

Walking: 45 mins, difficult
Train: Exeter, 25km
Extras: Little Hound Tor Stone Circle

ⓘ Small, dammed plunge pool in brook at edge of moor. Shallow (1m) but set beneath flat rock rapids with nice picnicking grass alongside. Paddling for children. Sheltered and balmy in summer. Park in South Zeal.

▶ From south (Ramsley) end of village follow lane, dir Throwleigh. After 1km, at telephone box, take R lane. After 600m turn R, up dead-end lane and continue on wooded trackway up hill for another 600m. You come through a gate into the moor. Follow wall to L for 200m and stream (Blackaton Brook) appears with Shilley Pool just below.

△ **15** River Taw behind Chapelton Station

North Devon
Tarka Trails

Tarka the Otter, one of Britain's best-loved nature stories, was set along the north Devon rivers of the Torridge and Taw. I followed the rivers, from highland pools to wooded river valleys, swimming in Tarka's paw-steps.

Henry Williamson was a disillusioned young man when he arrived on his racing motorcycle from London to live in a tiny cobb cottage on the north Devon coast. He had just returned from the horrors of the First World War, weary and nerve-wracked, at odds with his family and desperate to be a writer. He lived alone, hermit-fashion, tramping about the countryside, swimming in brooks and often sleeping out. The doors and windows of his new cottage were never closed, and his strange family of dogs, cats, gulls, buzzards and magpies were free to come and go as they pleased. This was to become the sanctuary for the real-life Tarka: an orphaned otter cub who took up refuge with Williamson.

High on north Dartmoor, the headwaters of the Torridge and the Taw provide an excellent vantage point to survey Williamson's famous 'Tarka Country'. Here on the East Okement, an important tributary of the Torridge, the army blew out a small but beautiful pool at Cullever Steps, just below Scarey Tor, as somewhere for servicemen to cool off during hot summers. It can still be reached via the decaying network of moorland military roads. As you bathe here, among the grazing wild ponies, Devonshire's rolling countryside unfolds like a soft counterpane below, with the steep wooded river valleys of the Torridge and the broader, gentler reaches of the Taw just discernible to the north.

At Halsdon Nature Reserve, ten miles away on the Torridge, the otter population is almost back to its pre-1950 levels. Historically Devon

△**15** Riverside thistles

△**14**

△**16** Otter after a swim

has been an international stronghold for otters, but in the 1950s and '60s their numbers crashed as industry and farming intensified. Watercourses became contaminated with chemicals and farm runoff. By the late 1960s the local otters were almost extinct. A massive clean-up over the last thirty years has had a major impact on the health of all British rivers. Now at Halsdon you'll see white-legged damselflies, kingfishers, sand martins, herons, dippers and grey wagtails. There are even freshwater pearl mussels.

Halsdon won't welcome you to swim as it disturbs the wildlife, but downstream, near Little Torrington, you can wade across the river at the old ford near Undercleave. This is a remote spot and the river here runs wide, fast and shallow under a tunnel of tall trees. Great Torrington Common, below Great Torrington town, is an accessible stretch of fast-flowing, shady river with some deeper holes. It was here that Tarka learned to swim, to play and to hunt and also first encountered the poachers with their trap lights like 'little moons which he could touch and bite'.

Seven miles to the east the Taw is a very different kind of river and runs through flatter, more open countryside. Behind the remote Chapelton Station on the Barnstaple line you'll find a meadow and footbridge with good access to the river from open fields. The river is wide, flowing across smooth gravels with a perfect current against which you can swim.

Bathing in the rivers and streams of this area was one of Henry Williamson's greatest pleasures. He brought up his children at Shallowford, six miles to the east, and spent much of his time in the river Bray fishing or swimming. He describes in his memoirs lying still in the golden gravels of the ford, watching the clear, cold water foaming over his body. It took him a long time to get over his experiences of the war and feel at peace with his world but it was at moments like this, he said, that he could finally feel 'a part of the great stream of life'.

North Devon Tarka Trails

14 Cullever Steps

Town: Okehampton, 7km
Grid ref: SX 606924
Postcode: EX20 1QR (1.2km SE)

Water quality: A+
Depth/size: plunge, paddle

Walking: 15 mins, moderate
Train: Exeter, 35km
Extras: Walk to East Okement Head

ⓘ Small plunge pool in narrow rocky valley below Scarey Tor. Some grass for picnics and large rocks for sunbathing. Small waterfalls. 1.5m deep. 15m long.

▶ From Okehampton town centre traffic lights follow red army signs south to 'Camp'. After 2.5km arrive at T-junction on moor (army camp on R). Turn L. This is the old army 'ring road' with many potholes. 1.2km up and over hill brings you to rough track off to L, 50m before the bridge/ford. Park and follow track down, stream on your R, to another ford 700m. Follow stream another 300m down to pool.

15 Chapelton Station, Taw

Town: Barnstable, 8km
Grid ref: SS 582261
Postcode: EX37 9EB (300m SE)

Water quality: A
Depth/size: swim, current

Walking: 5 mins, easy
Train: Chapelton, 200m
Extras: Shallowford, Williamson's home

ⓘ Open river meadows by footbridge behind small railway halt on Barnstaple line. The Taw is large and wide here (50m across), fast flowing, but mainly shallow (1m). Good for swimming against the current but be careful. Popular fishing river so be discreet and respect fishermen who may be there.

▶ Chapelton is small station 8km south of Barnstaple on A377 (dir Exeter). Station is on L, after the chapel, easy to miss. Park and walk through gate to L of station building, over railway line, across field to footbridge. Bathe downstream of bridge. 1m deep in places.

16 Great Torrington

Town: Great Torrington
Grid ref: SS 582261
Postcode: EX37 9EB (300m SE)

Water quality: A
Depth/size: swim, current, paddle

Walking: 5 mins, easy
Train: Umberleigh, 10km
Extras: Tarka Trail cycle tour

ⓘ The Torridge at Torrington Common is fast flowing and pebbly but mainly shallow (1m) with some deeper holes. Woody, steep and wide the river is the setting for many of Tarka's adventures.

▶ From Great Torrington go downhill on A386, dir Okehampton. After 1km park in lay-by R, by sharp bend before bridge and opposite junction with A3214 on L. Follow track into woods, downstream, and onto the steep banks of Torrington Common. Also access from near Little Torrington, 2km further on A386. From village take dead-end lane 3km east towards Hollam, Undercleave and downhill to old ford (SS 518166).

△ **17** River Barle on the way to Cow Castle

Exmoor and River Barle

Heather-topped hills, bracken-covered combes, tumbling waterfalls and wooded river valleys prompted the Victorians to name the magnificent scenery and quiet charm of Exmoor the 'Little Switzerland of England'.

Straddling north Devon and Somerset, this ancient landscape of iron-age barrows, hut circles and high flat hills was popular with the first humans to colonise Britain after the ice age. Exmoor is now Britain's least-visited National Park but contains several small and delightful swimming rivers.

An old friend Hue – and his dog Felix – had offered to take me to one of their swimming holes near Cow Castle, a pre-historic hill fort on a remote part of the River Barle. We met at Simonsbath, an auspicious-sounding place for the job at hand, and dropped down through Birchcleave woods to the river. The Barle runs in a narrow vale lined with bright orange asphodels for much of the two miles to Cow Castle. It is a shallow stream that twists and turns between avenues of birch and the ruins of old mine workings. As it reaches the conical hill of the fort it deepens and slows into a pool.

Swimming against the current of this small buffeting stream was harder than we had anticipated and soon we had a competition going to see who could beat the river and make it upstream. We then tried to out-swim the dog. Once we were all thoroughly exhausted we ran up to the top of the castle knoll and collapsed on the grass, the wet dog panting and the evening sun glowing low.

From here the course of the Barle winds its way another two miles before it reaches Sherdon Hutch and Landacre Bridge. These

△ **18** Withypool, downstream of Landacre Bridge

△ **18**

△ **18** Dandelions by the River Barle

△ **19**

have long been popular Exmoor bathing and picnicking spots with shallows by the bridge and a deeper hole at the confluence of the Sherdon brook upstream. According to Hue, locals believe there is a hot spring somewhere along its course near here that makes the water especially warm. Perhaps the hot spring was broken the next day because the water was pretty invigorating at Landacre. Despite this, several families had taken up positions along the bank. At Withypool, a few miles further on, barbeques and picnics were in full swing and a small flotilla of inflatable boats was in operation.

At Tarr Steps there were even more people. The clapper bridge here is truly impressive. Constructed from megalithic flat stones laid end to end and propped up on boulders, it is one of the best-known monuments on Exmoor and several theories claim it dates from the Bronze Age, although others date it to around 1400AD. One myth has it that the Devil built it to win a bet and swore he would kill anyone who tried to cross it. To test his curse the villagers sent a cat across. That was promptly vaporised so the terrified locals sent the parson across next. Although the Devil swore and intimidated him, the parson swore back and finally the Devil succumbed and allowed people to pass, except when he wanted to sunbathe.

Between, above and below the flagstones, children were chasing minnows, skimming stones and getting thoroughly wet. I decided to find some peace and headed upstream a couple of miles through the beautiful National Nature Reserve. The woods here are internationally renowned for their mosses, liverworts and lichens, including a type of moss found in burrows, which appears to glow in the dark. They are also home to the rare barbastelle bat, which breeds in the cracks of old trees. Feeling wonderfully relaxed away from everyone I found a perfect pool, not too deep, some way down from a footbridge. Here I swam, disturbed by no one, not even the Devil.

Exmoor and River Barle

17 Cow Castle, Barle

Town: Simonsbath, 3km
Grid ref: SS 793375
Postcode: TA24 7LA (800m E)

Water quality: A
Depth/size: plunge, current

Walking: 45 mins, moderate
Train: Barnstaple, 25km
Extras: Exmoor Forest Inn, Simonsbath

ⓘ Deepish, smallish pool (10m x 20m x 1.5m deep) in the babbling river Barle in wild scenery beneath the ancient hill fort 'Cow Castle'. Grass banks, orange asphodels. Long walk from car.

▶ From the Forest Inn in Simonsbath, cross the road and follow the footpath bearing R through woods and out on to moor by river (200m). Follow path for 2.4km along beautiful river valley with old mines and avenues of trees. Pool is just a deeper section of river, below Cow Castle and immediately below a river 'gate'. You can continue on to Sherdon's Hutch from here.

18 Sherdon and Landacre

Town: Withypool, 7km
Grid ref: SS 806361
Postcode: TA24 7LA (1km SE)

Water quality: A
Depth/size: plunge, paddle

Walking: 5 mins, moderate
Train: Barnstaple, 25km
Extras: Royal Oak Inn, Withypool

ⓘ Small junction pool of Barle and Sherdon, upstream from popular paddling at Landacre Bridge. Open and sunny with plenty of grass but some bog.

▶ From A361 South Molton follow Withypool road 10km. 1km after Sportsman's Inn, turn L. After 2km turn onto track on L and park at bottom (800m) on grassy hillside. Sherdon Hutch is small junction pool 200m below, beneath a river 'gate'. You can also park at Landacre Bridge, (SS 816361) further down the lane, good for paddling and inflatables, and walk up. Withypool village also has good paddling, 6km downstream (SS 844354).

19 Tarr Steps, Barle

Town: Withypool, 7km
Grid ref: SS 860327
Postcode: TA22 9PY (800m NW)

Water quality: A
Depth/size: plunge, current

Walking: 20 mins, moderate
Train: Tiverton Parkway, 25km
Extras: Tarr Farm Inn, Tarr Steps

ⓘ Ancient stone 'clapper' bridge, very popular with children for paddling. Deeper pool of Barle about 20 mins upstream through woods. Good food at pub.

▶ From Withypool follow signs to Dulverton. Turn R on to B3223 (Winsford Hill) and after 4km turn R at crossroads, dir Liscombe and signed Tarr Steps. Park after 2km and walk down to river. After admiring bridge, head upriver on woodland path 1.5km, into forest and then out on fields to find deeper pools below footbridge. River path continues, if you wish, to Withypool (4km) returning by Two Moors Way.

△ **21** Rockford Pools on the East Lyn

North Exmoor and the Lyn

Lynmouth was the site of one of the most devastating floods in British history. The upper reaches of the River Lyn sweep through the peaceful Doone Valley, the setting for the famous novel *Lorna Doone*. There are good pools and waterfalls along its entire course.

The River Lyn took on ferocious force on the night of the 15th August 1952. An intense tropical storm rolled in from the Atlantic and dropped nine inches of rain on the already waterlogged moors. None of the rivers could cope and banks burst all over Exmoor. At Hawkridge the massive Tarr Steps were washed a hundred yards downstream, and in another village a row of ten cottages were completely swept away. But the worst devastation was on the Lyn at Lynmouth where an avalanche of churning trees and boulders destroyed over 100 buildings and 29 bridges. 38 cars were washed out to sea and in total 34 people died. New evidence now suggests that the extreme weather events of August 1952 may have been a result of top secret cloud seeding experiments taking place at the time off the Devon coast.

As you stand at Watersmeet, a Victorian fishing lodge, now a quaint National Trust-run tea shop, it's sobering to think of the force of this water and debris piling down the hillside. Yet, ironically, the Lyn has a long history of water power. In 1890 it was one of the first places in the world to install a hydroelectric generator which provided lighting and powered an ice-maker for the local fishing crews.

△ **20** Watersmeet waterfalls

△ **22** Felix

△ **22** Hue's boots

The main attractions at Watersmeet now are the simple waterfalls and woodland walks. The closest falls are impressive and popular so if you're not shy why not take a dip right there? If you'd prefer to be a little more discreet then follow the river path a couple of miles upstream to the little-known Long Pool, a deep narrow gorge which can be found in the woods beneath the path. Further on the path continues to Rockford and before you get there you'll find several more pools with small cliffs to jump from. As I was exploring I met two families kitted out with wetsuits and rubber dinghies. They had spent much of the afternoon playing in these shady pools and said it was more fun than being on the nearby beach.

In Rockford you'll find the well-known brewery and real ales of the Rockford Inn. Follow the river further upstream to Malmsmead to discover the notorious setting of *Lorna Doone: an Exmoor Romance* by R. D. Blackmoore, one of the bestselling books of all time. The church at nearby Oare is where the novel's famous conclusion was set.

This land of murder and outlaws has tumbling streams and dense woods. Wildlife abounds throughout the area. Red deer, ponies and sheep graze freely, watched over by falcons, buzzards and even the rare merlin. Cloud Farm is a great place to stay, with pony trekking, a campsite and river paddling in the Badgworthy, a tributary of the Lyn. But on a hot summer day Deer Park Pool is the place to be, a mile further up the stream. As you come out of the woods and into an open grassland clearing you'll find a circular plunge pool flowing under a large ash tree. Although small, it's deep enough for a good splash, as my friend, Hue, and his dog, Felix, demonstrated. The path continues on and up to more Doone country on Brendon Moor, or you may prefer to return to the farm shop for one of their famous *après*-swim cream teas.

North Exmoor and the Lyn

20 Long Pool, Watersmeet

Town: Lynmouth, 3km
Grid ref: SS 753483
Postcode: EX35 6NT (1km E)

Water quality: A
Depth/size: plunge, swim

Walking: 20 mins, moderate
Train: Barnstaple, 25km
Extras: www.watersmeet.org.uk

ⓘ Watersmeet is a famous National Trust area of wooded river walks. There is a waterfall with small plunge pools by the teashop but 1.5km further on is Long Pool, a rather eerie long ravine and pool overgrown with ferns and oaks, set under a waterfall. Very deep, 50m long.

▶ Watersmeet is 2km south of Lynmouth on the A39. From Watersmeet House (shop, tea room) follow riverside trail upstream, through woods and onto open hillside (1km). Another 500m brings you back into the woods and, about 100m after entering, you'll find Long Pool, a narrow cataract beneath a series of waterfalls, beneath you.

21 Rockford Pools

Town: Lynmouth, 5km
Grid ref: SS 753482
Postcode: EX35 6PT (500m NW)

Water quality: A
Depth/size: plunge, jump

Walking: 10 mins, moderate
Train: Barnstaple, 28km
Extras: Rockford Inn

ⓘ Rockford is tiny hamlet next to the tumbling wooded East Lyn above Watersmeet. Good real ale pub and series of small pools with low rock cliffs to jump from. Shady and dark, but good fun.

▶ From the Rockford Inn (www. therockfordinn.com, own brewery, wood stove and good food) cross the road and footbridge and follow river's R bank 500m downstream into woods. Drop down to the stream to find series of small black pools, up to 2m deep, with rocky ledges. 200m further down is a waterfall. The Long Pool swim (see entry, left) is 300m below. The walk continues and connects to Watersmeet.

22 Badgworthy Pool

Town: Malmsmead, 2km
Grid ref: SS 793454
Postcode: EX35 6NU (2.3km N)

Water quality: A
Depth/size: plunge

Walking 20 mins, moderate
Train: Barnstaple, 25km
Extras: Cloud Farm farm shop

ⓘ Charming but small plunge pool underneath shallow waterfall and big tree in popular Doone Valley woodland walk. Further shallow pools and paddling at farm and campsite. Setting for *Lorna Doone*. Teashop.

▶ Malmsmead is a tiny village off A39 Lynmouth Minehead road and is at the heart of Doone country. Park here or drive 1km up to Cloud Farm campsite to use their shop or campsite. From here cross footbridge, follow path 1km/20 mins upstream until woods clear and path bears R up onto moor. On L, under a lip of bank, find small pool by large tree.

△ **23** Colber Bridge on the Dorset Stour

Dorset Stour and Somerset Brue

The meandering rivers of Thomas Hardy's Wessex twist and turn through lush pastures and cider-growing levels. Blossoms line the Somerset Brue in spring and yellow water lilies fill the Dorset Stour in summer.

Camping in fields close to the River Stour I awoke to a glorious morning mist, dew-clad spider webs hanging in the dried husks of cow parsley and tall brown bulrushes lining the banks. After sipping at a hot mug of tea, I walked up to Colber Bridge on the common beneath Sturminster Newton. With little sign of life from the village above, I slid down the muddy bank and into the cool water. The shadow of gudgeon darted through the murk and the odd weed tickled me as I swam under the bridge and down towards Bather's Island, the site of the old river swimming club.

Sturminster Newton is situated at an historic fording point of the Stour as it runs down through the Blackmore Vale, classic Dorset dairy country. It was at Colber Bridge that Thomas Hardy and his wife Emma spent their happiest years walking and swimming by the river. Their friend English poet William Barnes, also lived nearby for many years and wrote about the 'cloty Stour' – filled with its yellow water lilies and arrowhead much as it is today – in his *Poems of Rural Life in the Dorset Dialect*, written in thick, wonderful, old Dorset tongue.

△ 25

△ 23

△ 25 Daisies in the churchyard

'An' zwallows skim
the water, bright

Wi' whirlèn froth,
in western light;

Wi' whirlèn stwone,
an' streamèn flour,

Did goo the mill
by cloty Stour.'

William Barnes, 1862

Another popular Dorset Stour swimming hole is ten miles downstream at Pamphill towards Wimborne Minster. Here an old Roman ford, footbridge and weir create a large space for swimmers to paddle and play. Upstream the waters are wider and deeper.

Like many other southern English rivers, the Stour's wildlife suffered a great decline with the intensification of dairy farming in the 1970s. Lapwing, snipe and redshank all became rare. The river today is much recovered, but a new project – organised by the rural heritage charity, Common Ground – is keeping the issue of river ecology in people's minds with a project to make music inspired by the river.

If river music is your thing then St Peter's Church, set alongside the River Brue at Lydford, is noted for its choral tradition. Dorothy, an energetic, silver-haired woman in her 60s, has swum here since she was a child. 'I loved listening to the choir practise as we glided past the blossoms in spring. It was like a natural baptism.'

The smell of ozone from the tumbling water and the swooping manoeuvres of the damselflies are sure signs of how clean the river is today. Directly below the old weir is a small pool where children paddle and play. On warm weekends in summer you might find the neat lawns of the churchyard laid out with deckchairs and towels and a mixture of swimmers and spectators, of all ages, jumping in from the bridge or swimming breaststroke back and forth along the blossomed reach, pulling themselves out between the two cherry trees, then sipping Earl Grey tea on the grass.

Somerset literally means 'land of the summer people', because the area could not be populated in the winter due to the great sea floods that inundated the levels. Lydford stands on the edge of this flood plain. From here its only a couple of miles to Baltonsborough Flights, another swimming hole, where the river drops down a weir via a large pool before beginning its journey to sea, through the heady blossoms of cider groves, willow and teasel.

Dorset Stour and Somerset Brue

23 Colber Bridge

Town: Sturminster Newton
Grid ref: ST 783143
Postcode: DT10 1EG (200m W)

Water quality: B
Depth/size: swim, dive

Walking: 5 mins, easy
Train: Sherborne, 14km
Extras: Sturminster Newton Museum

ℹ An open stretch of the Stour with grassy fields by elegant white wrought-iron Colber Bridge. A little weedy and slow, but clean and deep. Long swims. Just upstream from overgrown 'Bather's Island'.

▶ Park in town car park and walk up hill to the High Street, over road and into The Row by the library and village hall. At end of the cul-de-sac (100m) go through iron gate and follow the footpath down the hill (100m) and straight over (50m) to find Colber Bridge on an open stretch of meadow. Long swim in either direction. Local museum has working mill and charts old world country life.

24 Pamphill

Town: Wimborne Minster
Grid ref: ST 996001
Postcode: BH21 4EE (300m S)

Water quality: B
Depth/size: swim, dive, paddle

Walking: 5 mins, easy
Train: Bournemouth/Poole 10km
Extras: National Bike Trail No. 25

ℹ A wide stretch of mature river at old ford with weir, bridge and long upstream swimming stretch. Good access and riverside walks. Weedy in places, but clean.

▶ From Wimborne Minster town centre take B3082 dir Blandford Forum. After 500m, at hospital, turn L down lane dir Pamphill. 1km on L find car park and river. Immediately below is weir, fun to play above or below. Swim by bridge or head upstream 500m to find another good access point at overgrown site of old Roman road ford. Banks are otherwise quite steep. (Lane leads on 4km to lovely old bridge at White Mill.)

25 West Lydford

Town: Castle Cary
Grid ref: ST 564319
Postcode: TA11 7DH

Water quality: B
Depth/size: swim, dive, paddle

Walking: 5 mins, easy
Train: Castle Cary, 8km
Extras: Glastonbury town and tor, 9km

ℹ A pretty 100m stretch of river running alongside church lawns between old bridge and weir. Gravel bed by weir, though a bit mushy from old leaves by bridge. Access from either bank of weir. Rope swing. 1.5m deep by weir. 2m under bridge.

▶ West Lydford is just off the A37, near the junction B3153 (Lydford-on-Fosse). Footpath runs through churchyard to weir and then footbridge. Also access via track on opposite bank. Follow river 2.5km via Tootle Bridge Farm to find Baltonsborough Flights (ST 548338) weir and pool near Catsham (200m NW of BA6 8PQ).

△ **28** The weir at Claverton, River Avon

North Somerset's Frome and Avon

The Somerset Frome near Bath is the home of one of the country's last surviving river-swimming clubs, with stories of camping, galas and wild-swimming parties.

The Farleigh and District Swimming Club occupies a great sweep of south-facing meadow by an old diving frame and gravel-bedded weir pool on the Frome. With over 2,000 members, people come here from far and wide to experience real swimming and to sunbathe on the grassy banks.

The club was founded in 1933 during the great boom in British river swimming. The village was already popular with the people of Trowbridge a few miles away who would walk over to Farleigh at the weekend to swim, visit the castle and have a drink at the Hungerford Arms. The four Greenhill brothers owned the farm on the opposite side of the bank and also loved to swim. One day they invited some of these regular bathers to form a swimming club and for the next 20 years the club flourished. Summers saw a regular group who would camp out on the banks, rise at six for an early-morning dip and then go off haymaking for the day. There were Wednesday evening swimming galas, great bonfires and general summer antics, all with the enthusiastic support of the Greenhills.

△ 28

△ 26

'Britain's only hot spring waters are now available for bathing again after a 28-year closure. The water that bubbles up from the ground at Bath fell as rain on the Mendip Hills many thousands of years ago. It is returning to the surface after percolating down through limestone aquifers to a depth of about 4km where geothermal energy has raised its temperature to 64°C.'
www.thermalbathspa.com

In more recent years the club has swapped banks and the new landlords are just as enthusiastic and they run a campsite and tea shop a mile upstream. This river is a beautiful setting for a summer afternoon with children swimming among the moorhens and alder roots and the spray from the weir catching the floating dandelion seeds. There are no galas or bonfires here anymore but the big-hearted welcome still exists.

Two miles upstream at Tellisford the landowners have also been modernising with a sensitive eye for wild swimmers. A beautiful weir pool is located a little way up from a medieval packhorse bridge among wide fields and an odd Second World War bunker – apparently this was a position on the 'Somerset Stop Line Green' where the British planned to defend the country against an attack coming from the south coast. This weir, like the one at Farleigh, was constructed in the early nineteenth century to power the village mill. Although it stopped working many generations ago, the weir pool has been saved by a local project to generate 60kW from the renovated mill chase – enough to power the whole village. This is an exciting green initiative which has preserved the weir pool, provides a more stable supply of electricity than wind and is less unsightly than a turbine.

Weir power is fairly common in this area. Claverton (Warleigh) Weir, five miles downstream and on the outskirts of Bath, forms a long, meandering waterfall across the River Avon. It looks a little like a miniature Victoria Falls stretching into the distance. At over one hundred yards long it was built in 1810 to power a pump that would lift water from the river to the nearby Kennet and Avon Canal. It has created a huge pool in the Avon, and a spectacularly wide waterfall. Children play under the dam and in the shallows. Adults can take a long swim above the weir and up the Avon, for the best part of a mile.

North Somerset's Frome and Avon

26 Farleigh Hungerford, Frome

Town: Trowbridge
Grid ref: ST 806577
Postcode: BA3 6RS

Water quality: B
Depth/size: swim, dive

Walking: 1 min, easy
Train: Trowbridge, 5km
Extras: Castle and campsite

ⓘ One of the country's last river-swimming clubs occupies a pleasant, deep but narrow stretch of the Frome above a weir. Lawns and steps into water, about 1–2.5m deep with gravelly bed. Car parking in field very close by. Changing huts and portaloo.

▶ Farleigh Hungerford is on the A366 between Trowbridge and A36. The field is through a gate on the L, at the corner before (E of) the two humpback bridges. Drive across field and park. Occasionally there is a club member who will take a fee. Stowford Farm camping and B&B just upstream (www.stowfordmanorfarm. co.uk, 01225 775919).

27 Tellisford, Frome

Town: Trowbridge
Grid ref: ST 806554
Postcode: BA3 6RL (300m S)

Water quality: B
Depth/size: swim, dive

Walking: 1 min, easy
Train: Trowbridge, 5km
Extras: Packhorse bridge

ⓘ Sloping green field by large weir pool. Lovely pastoral aspect with trees and hillside. 1m deep by weir wall but much deeper (3m) just upstream under fallen tree. Popular with local kids and sometimes there is litter. Riverbed dry downstream due to hydro extraction.

▶ On A366 heading W from Trowbridge turn R after 3km on B3109 dir Rode. After 2km, at crossroads, look out for small dead end lane R, signed Tellisford. Park at end (1km) and walk down to river and medieval bridge. Follow path upstream 300m to old pillbox by weir.

28 Claverton Weir, Avon

Town: Bath
Grid ref: ST 792643
Postcode: BA2 7BH (100m S)

Water quality: C
Depth/size: swim, dive, paddle

Walking: 10 mins, moderate
Train: Bath, 4km
Extras: Pump house, Bike Path No. 24

ⓘ 100m long weir in wonderful valley of the Avon. Meadow, old ferry crossing steps, long deep water stretches. Shallow paddling areas above weir, play areas under weir near bank. Water generally clean despite Environment Agency rating. Popular. Follow A36 out of Bath (or cut across via university campus).

▶ After 3km on A36 Claverton hamlet is on R. Turn L down narrow Ferry Lane. Park on lane then walk to bottom (old Claverton Pump Station), cross into big field, bear R to come to weir. Museum is sometimes open (www.claverton.org). No approach by village of Warleigh on opposite bank.

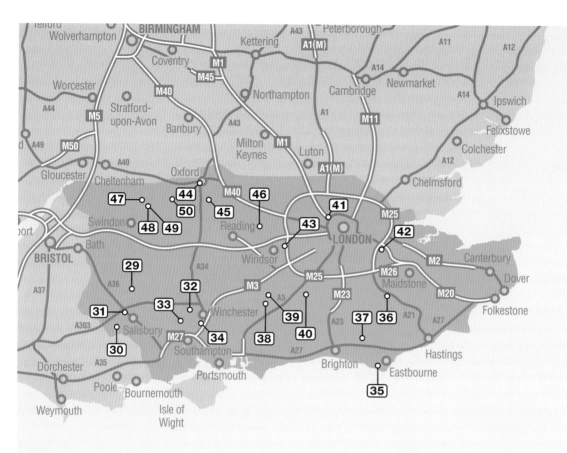

Highlights

29–31 Tiny river pools beneath small chutes in the streams that drain Salisbury Plain and Stonehenge

33 White shingle beach and dancing water buttercups line the crystal-clear chalk streams that drain Hampshire's Watership Down

35 These 'lost' river meanders are set in the spectacular Cuckmere Haven

37 Hire rowboats from the Anchor Inn and swim along two miles of Sussex's most remote and rural river

38 A popular inland beach, set in ancient Surrey heathland, built by the Bishop of Winchester in the sixteenth century

41 One of Britain's oldest and most famous bathing ponds, these pools were constructed 400 years ago to provide London with drinking water through hollowed-out elm tree pipes

42 A pretty village just off the M25 where children play in the ford

44 In the centre of Oxford, not far from the station, the riverside at Port Meadow inspired Lewis Carroll in the opening of *Alice in Wonderland*

45–46 Beautiful stretches of the River Thames that provided the setting for *Three Men in a Boat* and *Wind in the Willows*

47 Cheese Wharf, a deep bend in the young River Thames, great for swimming and once the location for barges loaded with Gloucestershire cheese

49 A beautiful weir pool, lined by willow trees and rope swings with grassy National Trust lawns for sunbathing

South

The ancient downlands of Wiltshire and Hampshire create the world renowned chalk streams of the Wylye, Test and Itchen – shallow, clear and white. Great father Thames flows through Oxfordshire to the north and is filled with literary association. The Surrey and Sussex hills are surprisingly rich in secret wooded pools and even London has some wild-swimming gems.

△ **29** Pool on Hampshire Avon at Figheldean

Salisbury Plains and Wiltshire Chalk Streams

Salisbury Plain is the headwater for three chalk streams – the Nadder, Wylye and Hampshire Avon – that all descend on Salisbury. Percolating from the hills, they are fabulously clean, clear and cold!

I arrived at the Avon in Figheldean, just south of Stonehenge, to find bikinis hung on a Morris Minor, a picnic hamper spread out under a willow tree and a mother and her three children paddling and shrieking in cold glee. This is a beautiful pool above a footbridge at the end of a little lane by the church. The water is exceptionally clean and clear and roars in over a simple sluice-type affair, first into a deep hole, and then over white pebble shallows and flint sand banks with views out over hay fields.

Two young men in shorts and wellies had also just arrived from across the fields and were racing each other to be first to dive into the deep pool beneath the small waterfall weir. Elizabeth, an elderly resident of the village, was spectating from a deckchair, calling out comments and clapping at all the action. In the old days, she said, the pool was always packed in the summer, particularly with servicemen from the airbases. During the war there were Land Army girls here too. Some said their naked bathing was distracting the village from the war effort and the local policeman, who also ran the village swimming lessons, ordered that bathers should be suitably clothed for decorous bathing.

△ **31**

△ **29** Swimwear drying on a Morris Minor

△ **30** Mother swan and cignets

The Nadder, some miles away, is a much quieter, smaller stream splashing down through the uplands of the Cranborne Chase. I was quickly lost among the narrow lanes searching for a public footpath that might give bankside access. There, on a hill brow, with a sign pointing down through a billowing wheat field to a little bridge, I finally found a tiny map-marked public right of way.

The riverside is neatly mown and cordoned off, clearly prepared for some very well organised fishing. I dare say fishermen would not welcome wild swimmers so I followed the footpath gingerly, not wishing to disturb the peace, but I saw no one, save a dipper and a wagtail, and I arrived alone, hot but delighted, as the river widened into a clear shelving pool behind shrubs. A chute of the purest spring water poured in over an old hatch. Making a neat pile of clothes on a fishing bench, I climbed down the soft grass bank, tiptoed along the deepening riverbed and swam breaststroke into the pool. Pebbles of whites, greys and reds formed a wobbling mosaic on the cool river-pool floor.

The third chalk stream – the Wylye – runs in between the Nadder and Avon. I had initially been attracted to Steeple Langford by a series of lakes I spied from the main road late one evening. What were once gravel pits are now a nature reserve and just as I was preparing to head home disappointed that a silent dip wasn't allowed I spied a tiny lawn with a bench, opposite the nature reserve entrance, and a small sign: 'Entry to the pool is prohibited to those unable to swim.' With these magic words a small but beautiful pool appeared, turning a silver green hue in the fading evening light! A mother swan was collecting some final weedy titbits before tucking up her cygnets for the evening and the church warden was cycling by on her bike, making home for supper. I tiptoed excitedly over the white shingle and waded into the pool. Here, floating like Ophelia, I lay in a perfect stillness, starring up at an indigo sky and the first stars of the evening.

Salisbury Plains and Wiltshire chalk streams

29 Figheldean, Avon

Town: Amesbury
Grid ref: SU 151475
Postcode: SP4 8JL (200m W)

Water quality: A
Depth/size: current, dive, paddle
Walking: 1 min, easy

Train: Salisbury, 14km
Extras: Stonehenge, 5km

ⓘ Medium pool, 20m x 60m, with chalk shingle in shallows and deep section (2–3m) beneath a small weir into which people jump. Footbridge and easy parking. Limited grass for picnics. Cold water.

▶ At Amesbury (only 2km from Stonehenge and on A303) take A345 N, dir Pewsey. After 5km turn R dir Figheldean. After 600m turn L into small lane. Park at end. Footbridge is ahead with pool on R. As well as Stonehenge there are a wide variety of walks on the Plains and army ranges above here, though check for access first.

30 Teffont Evias, Nadder

Town: Salisbury
Grid ref: ST 987301
Postcode: SP3 5RW (400m SE)

Water quality: A
Depth/size: plunge, paddle
Walking: 15 mins, moderate

Train: Salisbury, 16km
Extras: Fovant Down, 4km

ⓘ Small, secret pool under hatches, public right of way, but on well-maintained fishing beat so don't swim if fishermen there.

▶ Take A36 west dir Warminster. At Wilton roundabout (4km) L on A30 dir Shaftesbury. At Barford St Martin (4km) R by church to B3089 dir Dinton. After 6km (1km after Dinton) turn L (dir Tisbury). Down to lake (L), up hill and 1km to find footpath sign L on brow of hill. Follow path down through field to stream, across bridge and along river 400m. (Public right of way actually marked as river L on maps, but now seems to have been diverted river R.)

31 Steeple Langford, Wylye

Town: Salisbury
Grid ref: SU 037371
Postcode: SP3 4NJ (300m S)

Water quality: A
Depth/size: plunge, paddle
Walking: 1 min, easy

Train: Salisbury, 12km
Extras: Langford Lakes, wildlife

ⓘ A small, cold, shelving pool with deep section (3m). By bench and lawn behind hedge but visible from road bridge. White chalk shingle riverbed. 30m x 30m.

▶ Steeple Langford is 13km W of Salisbury on the A36 (dir Warminster). Take sign for 'The Langfords' and turn L into Steeple Langford down Duck Street. Nature Reserve is 500m on L, just over bridge. Pool and lawn is opposite, on R through gate. Hourly bus from Salisbury (X4, X5, X6), Monday to Saturdays, 7am–6pm. Nature reserve opposite with visitor centre (www.wiltshirewildlife.org).

△ **33** The white shingle banks of the Test at Houghton

Hampshire Chalk Streams: Test and Itchen

The wide braids of the River Test run through some of the least developed parts of the South East. Wily and fast, the stream picks its way through the most tranquil parts of Hampshire as it heads for the sea.

Watership Down, that chalk downland immortalised by Richard Adams, is the headwater for the river Test. These were the hills down which Pipkin and Hazel fled, first from the bulldozers, then from Efrafan's rabbit soldiers, before jumping onto a punt moored on the river at Laverstoke. Like the Salisbury chalk streams, public access to the bankside is rare, with fishing rights charging out at up to £1,000 per day. But at Chilbolton Cow Common, near Cherwell Priory, there has been public access since ancient times.

The little footbridges here are a magnet for families paddling and playing Pooh sticks on a hot summer day, but as I arrived at seven o'clock on an early evening in June the last of the picnickers were leaving. The clear waters of the chalk stream are the home for many unique plants and as I dipped in the shallow waters it was like bathing in an underwater flower meadow. The long fronds of yellow starwort rippled in the current like buttercups and the white water's crowfoot waved like daisies. The downland mineral water teemed through my hair and made rivulets about my fingers.

The chalk shingles of these streams were laid down long ago. Coral reefs and sea plankton collected during the landscape's time as part

of an equatorial archipelago thousands of millions of years ago. Then the water would have been a balmy 30° Celcius but the temperature now is far from tropical – a chilly 15° Celcius. Rising from aquifers deep beneath the hills, the temperature remains remarkably constant throughout the year so that even on frosty winter mornings the Test is relatively warm, and it is famous for its steaming river mists. Then, a bath here feels almost balmy.

At Houghton, another favourite paddling location five miles away, a white shingle bay opens out onto a large shallow pool under a bridge where you can swim against the current. The old trackway crosses water meadows to John of Gaunt's deer park and the ancient yews at King's Somborne. The river course has changed much in the last three hundred years. In John's time new channels were being cut for the creation of 'floating' water meadows. A system of sluices encouraged the river to flood the fields, nourishing the grass and protecting it from frost to make possible earlier lambing and increased sheep stocking. It's now difficult to know which is the original river course and which an old irrigation path.

Running through nearby Winchester, the Itchen is another chalk stream that has been much altered by man. It was deepened for barge navigation in the eighteenth century but most of it has returned to shallows though there is still a deep pool under the little waterfall at Twyford. Just upstream the river is about one metre deep and good for a longer swim, if you don't mind occasionally scraping your knees.

A path follows the Itchen all the way to Winchester making a pleasant two-mile walk, despite the noisy motorway which passes overhead. The Twyford Downs, site of the road protests of the 1990s, are up on your right and you might like to take a dip in Tumbling Bay. Eventually you'll reach the water meadows of St Cross where there are also some deeper pools by the medieval hospital.

Hampshire chalk streams: Test and Itchen

32 Chilbolton Cow Common

Town: Stockbridge
Grid ref: SU 389402
Postcode: SO20 6BD

Water quality: A
Depth/size: paddle

Walking: 2 mins, easy
Train: Andover, 7km
Extras: Test Way, Watership Down

ⓘ Ancient rural common bounded by two arms of the Test. Two shallow pools by footbridge, white gravel, very clear and clean. Popular with children. Cold, about 15°C all year round.

▶ From A303, take A3057 S, dir Stockbridge. After 5km, just over river, turn R. 1km on, look out for L turn (Joy's Lane) to common with parking at the end. Take path on R, then bear L to footbridge (200m) and popular paddling spot. Continue across bridge further 500m to next footbridge. More shallow river downstream for 500m.

33 Houghton, Test

Town: Stockbridge
Grid ref: SU 343317
Postcode: SO20 6LX

Water quality: A
Depth/size: plunge, paddle, current

Walking: 5 mins, easy
Train: Mottisfont & Dunbridge, 7km
Extras: Mottisfont Abbey, NT

ⓘ A wide, white chalk bay at the end of bridleway in beautiful countryside. Water flowers in early summer (crowsfoot and water buttercup). Shelving white gravel bed. 1m deep under bridge with swift flow.

▶ Stockbridge is on the A30 close to Winchester (M3) or Andover (A303). From town centre take A30 (dir Salisbury) for 200m, past church and over bridge, turning immediately L, dir Houghton. 3km, you will find trackway on L, signed King's Somborne (and 'Private Road'), about 200m beyond telephone box. Find bridge and ford at end (200m). Mottisfont Abbey riverside gardens are 5km downstream (www.nationaltrust.org.uk).

34 Twyford, Itchen

Town: Winchester
Grid ref: SU 476256
Postcode: SO21 1NT (400m W)

Water quality: A
Depth/size: paddle, current, plunge

Walking: 10 mins, moderate
Train: Shawford, 500m
Extras: Bush House Inn, Ovington

ⓘ Deep, lined pool above footbridge and below hatch. 2m deep. Very clear, clean, though some concrete in bottom. Natural river stretch directly upstream (1m deep).

▶ From M3 (J11) southbound, follow B3335 1.5km to Twyford. Take sharp narrow R turn (Berry Lane). Park by church (200m) and continue over footbridge, then 500m along fence boundary eventually to pool with hatch/waterfall. 800m upstream, at third further footbridge, you'll find Tumbling Bay (SU 478263). Continue 1.5km to medieval St Cross, 1m deep swim by meadow though there is an overgrown 'no swimming' sign (SU 478278).

△ **37** River Ouse, outside Anchor Inn, above Barcombe Mills

Sussex Downs and Kent

The Sussex Downs – between the Ouse and the Cuckmere rivers – were the rural heartland of the Bloomsbury Group. Now, as then, the rivers provide beautiful wild-swimming, from the reaches of the upper Ouse to the warm lake-land meanders of the Cuckmere Vale.

The great winding paths of the river Cuckmere became separated from their stream in the nineteenth century when a bypass 'cut' was built to stop the vale-land meadows flooding. The abandoned curves are now warm, safe lagoons, ideal for paddling, rafting and swimming. With panoramic views of the Seven Sisters cliffs and the sea, this is a stunning location to combine some saltwater and freshwater swimming. How long the meanders will survive is now in doubt as there are plans to let the sea flood these flatlands again and return them to their original ecology.

Above the Vale and over the Downs is Charleston Farmhouse, where Vanessa Bell lived after her separation from her husband. From here she could walk to visit her sister, Virginia Woolf, at Rodmell, on the Ouse. The houses, and area, became the rural retreat of one of the most influential literary and artistic groups of the twentieth century, known for their love of nature and wild-swimming.

△ 36

△ 37

E. M. Forster, schooled and brought up in nearby Tonbridge, visited more than once. Himself known to wild swim with Rupert Brooke in Grantchester, one of Forster's more famous literary scenes is of Freddy, George and Mr Beebe rebelliously dipping in the Surrey 'Sacred Lake' in *A Room With a View*. Mocking the world of Edwardian manners and social codes, it symbolised the great liberation of thought and feeling that Forster and his contemporaries believed natural bathing provided. Forster grew up swimming in the Medway, fed by the dark waters of the Ashdown Forest – home of Winnie the Pooh – between Kent and Sussex. You can still swim in the Medway, near Penshurst Place, to this day. The banks of the river slope steeply into rich, clean and weed-free water. The peaty smell and brownish hue are flavoured by the Wealds of Kent. To swim here is to be infused with an elixir of leaf litter and pine cones.

If you do visit Virginia Woolf's Rodmell the Ouse there is no great place to swim. The straight, tidal channel has swampy edges and a slick current as it runs under a bleak, open sky and its lack of charm is not helped by being the site where, just a few hundred yards from her home, the writer chose to kill herself. Woolf had suffered from periods of manic depression throughout her creative and brilliant life. She felt she was going mad again and after months of suffering she did not believe she would ever recover.

Just north of Rodmell and Charleston, upstream on the Ouse, the open fields of Barcombe Mills are a perfect place for cricket, leapfrog and other riverside games. The Ouse here is deep with pretty grassy banks, ideal for cooling down after cartwheels or diving in for a long swim among the rushes.

The well-known Anchor Inn is nearby, just a mile upstream, at the bottom of a dead-end lane. You can hire one of its fleet of blue row boats or swim for over two miles through remote countryside, the spire of Isfield church the only building in sight for the entire journey.

Sussex Downs and Kent

35 Cuckmere Meanders

Town: Seaford
Grid ref: TV 519990
Postcode: BN25 4AD (500m S)

Water quality: A
Depth/size: paddle, swim

Walking: 15 mins, moderate
Train: Seaford, 4km
Extras: Seven Sisters cliffs and sea

ⓘ Wide, shallow, moderately warm oxbow lakes cut off from the main Cuckmere stream. Grass banks and chalky beds. Non tidal and no current. Safe and deep enough for swimming in some places. Stunning setting with option of sea swimming too.

▶ From Seaford follow A259 dir Eastbourne 4km. As you come down into the valley, cross the river and park near the visitor centre at Exceat. Follow the path down on the L side of the valley, via the meanders, rather than the R side, via the canal 'cut'. Depth and condition can vary. Vanessa Bell's home 4km (www.charleston.org.uk).

36 Ensfield Bridge, Medway

Town: Tonbridge
Grid ref: TQ 547453
Postcode: TN11 8RZ (200m N)

Water quality: B
Depth/size: swim

Walking: 5 mins, moderate
Train: Leigh, 1km
Extras: Penshurst Place and cycle route

ⓘ Open, sunny stretch of peaty brown river by country road. Steep banks but deep water make it good for a longer swim. About 400m of footpath access. Sometimes busy with fishermen.

▶ Ensfield Bridge is 1km S of Leigh (B245, B2027 6km W of Tonbridge) or 3km N of Bidborough (B2176). Park near bridge and swim upstream. Excellent National Cycle Route 12 also starts here. Also swim hole 5km upstream in fields behind Poundsbridge (TQ 533421). Popular with children, a deep hole for jumping, plus beach. Silty. 4km W of Bidborough and 2km S of Penshurst Place (www.penshurstplace.com).

37 Barcombe Mills, Ouse

Town: Lewes
Grid ref: TQ 435148
Postcode: BN8 5BT (200m E)

Water quality: B
Depth/size: swim, dive

Walking: 10 mins, moderate
Train: Lewes, 6km
Extras: Anchor Inn boats

ⓘ Fantastic 5km stretch of swimming on river Ouse. No current but clean, deep water. Boat hire. Steep banks.

▶ From Lewes, take the A26 north, dir Uckfield. After 4km turn L signed Barcombe Cross. Stop at car park on R for the Mills (1km). Take the track (turn R off lane) and find stile on R (100m). Take footpath alongside the sluices and stream, cross narrow footbridge then find wide-open field (300m). Anchor Inn upstream (2km), with swimming and boating for further 3km. Drive to Inn (www.anchorinnandboating.co.uk) via Barcombe Cross, 4km further on from car park (TQ 442160, BN8 5BS).

△ **40** Pools and meres under Surrey's North Downs

Surrey Hills: Frensham and the Silent Pool

I first glimpsed Frensham Great Pond on a fuggy summer afternoon with the smell of reeds and heath in the air and the crunch of dry heather underfoot. Placid and fat, dark columns of cumulus clouds were rising high above it and two clinker dinghies were moving languidly near a far bank.

You'd be forgiven for not being too excited about the prospect of natural swimming in Surrey, but it does have its wilder pockets. Strangely it's the most wooded county in England, which means less nitrates from farmers and less watershed pollution. Much of its downland is protected within an Area of Outstanding Natural Beauty and the ancient chalk ridgeway of the North Downs runs across its hills.

The clouds above me were on the turn, stacking up against the hills, the heathland pines deep green against the grey of a pre-storm sky as I slipped gingerly into the mauve waters of Frensham Great Pond. A cheery moorhen paddled happily some distance from me before she took up a frantic taxi across the waters, her feet dangling as she struggled to become airborne and the first rain began to fall. A kaleidoscope of concentric circles rippled across the glassy surface as I glided on through the cooling waters, the humidity purged from the day.

This shallow, warmish lake has two bays with natural sandy beaches marked out for swimming. Built as a fish pond by the Bishop of Winchester when he took up a prolonged stay at his nearby castle

△ 38

△ 38

△ 39

at Farnham in 1246 it was drained every five years to cleanse it and grow barley. The last time it was emptied, however, was in 1942, during the Second World War, as it had become a great moonlit landmark for the German bombers.

Frensham Little Pond is on the other side of the A287 and both ponds feed into the Wey which flows down into Tilford. This is a truly English scene with a cricket green and pub, river paddling above a ford and a bridge built by medieval monks. It's a perfect place to while away a summer afternoon with lunch and a paddle or swim – there is a rope swing below the weir and some deeper sections above the bridge.

Moving east there are several more wooded lakes. Bolder Mere on Ockham Common (Wisley, M25 J10) is a rare remnant of the heathland ponds that used to cover much of Surrey. It's an important site for dragonflies and damselflies, and also for the rare hobby – one of the few birds that can actually catch a dragonfly. Wildlife here is definitely the main priority – when two common tern chicks were found by the side of the lake people were asked to refrain from swimming too close to them. This is Site of Special Scientific Interest (SSSI) run by Surrey Wildlife Trust, so it's best to slip into the water silently and carefully, with a view to blending in.

Just outside Guildford, the Silent Pool, in a hollow beneath the escarpment of the Downs, is springfed from the chalk aquifers. Like other chalk streams it is very cold and very clear. Surrounded with vegetation and overhung by huge silver birches it was greatly admired by the poet Tennyson for the clarity of its water. I once tried to swim there during a very hot summer but it had completely dried up. More recently it was used as the film set for the skinny-dipping scene in *Hippie Hippie Shake* with Sienna Miller. Legend has it that a local woodcutter's daughter was bathing naked in the lake when she heard a horse and rider. With no time to cover her body she made for the deeper water, despite not being able to swim. She drowned and her ghost can be seen at midnight, wading through the waters.

Surrey Hills: Frensham and the Silent Pool

38 Frensham Great Pond

Town: Farnham
Grid ref: SU 846405
Postcode: GU10 3DS (1km S)

Water quality: B
Depth/size: paddle, swim

Walking: 2 mins, easy
Train: Farnham, 7km
Extras: Café, display, walks

ⓘ Huge sandy lake with small buoyed-off swimming area shelving to 1.5m deep and 50m wide. Forest and open heathland. Parking, café and small museum, Popular with young families.

▶ From Farnham take A287 S, dir Haslemere, for 5km. After Mariner's Hotel take second R into small wooded lane, dir Frensham Pond. Continue 1km to find L turn into woods. Follow car park round to lakeside. Café sells burgers. There is a second (quieter) swimming bay 100m beyond first. The L after Mariner's leads to Frensham Little Pond, no swimming.

39 Tilford, River Wey

Town: Farnham
Grid ref: SU 875433
Postcode: GU10 2BN (100m S)

Water quality: B
Depth/size: paddle, plunge

Walking: 2 mins, easy
Train: Farnham, 4km
Extras: Barley Mow on village green

ⓘ Shallow river and ford at confluence of two Weys. Quintessential village green, cricket matches and pub. Deeper below ford and upstream of bridge.

▶ From Farnham station and level crossing take Tilford road away from town centre and to R of Waverley Arms. After 4km, and one set of traffic lights, arrive at Tilford's traffic-light-controlled double bridge. Cross and bear R 100m to parking. River is behind, opposite side of green, beneath medieval single track bridge. People also known to swim on Wey navigation: Godalming, between Peasmarsh and Upper Ensted (SU 987452).

40 Silent Pool and Bolder Mere

Town: Albury
Grid ref: TQ 060486
Postcode: GU5 9BW

Water quality: A
Depth/size: plunge

Walking: 5 mins, easy
Train: Chilworth, 3km
Extras: Sherborne open farm

ⓘ Famous springfed pools, renowned for their clear waters, on edge of North Downs. Shallow, some weeds, but rather magical. Used for film sets. Can dry up in hot summers. Be discreet when swimming.

▶ Pools are located just off A25/A248 junction, 8km E of Guildford. From A3 southbound: exit for A247, continue 3km onto A25 then, after 3km, at dual carriageway, Silent Pool is immediately on L by Sherborne Farm. Bolder Mere is on Ockham Common (TQ 077584) A3 south, 600m after M25/A3 junction. Also the stepping stones on the River Mole at Boxhill Country Park (TQ 173513).

△ **41** Hampstead Mixed Bathing Pond, early morning

London and suburbs

Within London's great concrete sprawl there are a surprising number of hidden green oases, and efforts by local authorities to prohibit swimming have catalysed a number of campaigns to reclaim wild-swimming rights.

The three Hampstead Heath swimming ponds are probably the best known of central London's wild swims. The Mixed Pond is the closest to the tube and always rings with a holiday air. Groups loll about on the lawn, picnics are consumed, friends breast-stroke down the avenue of trees catching up on old news and gossip. The Men's pond is bigger and Ladies' ponds wilder, but both are a little more difficult to reach if you don't have a bike.

The ponds date back to the end of the seventeenth century when the Hampstead Waterworks Company damned the two brooks that drain the Heath, piping the water down to the city in hollowed out elm trees. When the 'New River' from Hertfordshire to Islington superseded the ponds they became important for recreation and a painting by Constable depicts people bathing at Hampstead as early as 1829.

Given this long tradition it's not surprising that the Hampstead Heath Winter Swimming Club was up in arms when health and safety officials told them they could no longer swim there in the winter months. The club, which includes several prominent public figures, won their case to swim in a landmark ruling in 2005. The judge spoke out in favour of 'individual freedom' and against the imposition of 'a grey and dull safety regime'. This 2005 ruling has inspired other swimmers to reclaim their London ponds too.

Bury Lake at the Aquadrome near Rickmansworth tube is one such example, long used by recreational swimmers, who happily co-habit

△ 42

△ 41

△ 43

with dinghy sailors, ducks, toy boaters and fishermen. Molly Fletcher shows 1960s photographs of the lake teeming with hundreds of people swimming and playing. 'There were no more or less sailing boats, swimmers of fishermen then,' she explains. 'No more or less blue–green algae.' An ardent campaign is seeking to have the 'no swimming' notices removed on this peaceful and enticing lake.

The growing cult of health and safety, compensation claims and the nanny state means many local authorities are unsure what to do with their many traditional swimming lakes. During the 1990s many decided to put up 'no swimming' signs, fearing expensive lawsuits. The spring-fed mere at Black Park Country Park near Uxbridge was closed, as was the sandy lake at Ruislip Lido. All the same, many hundreds of families do still swim and paddle here through the summer.

Gravel pits offer further opportunities for swimming near London. The Colne valley, along the M25 western corridor, provided much of the gravel for London's building boom in the twentieth century. These pits quickly filled with spring water and returned to nature, becoming beautiful wildlife reserves close to the heart of the city. The six-mile bike path from Rickmansworth to the Denham Country Park passes more than twenty gravel lakes and close to Staines there are even more. My favourites are around Wraysbury and Hythe, a four-mile mosaic of wooded island archipelagos, open water, grassland and scrub. These sites, now SSSIs, provide nationally important wetland habitats for wintering wildfowl, rare marigold, horned pondweed, tufted duck, gadwall and goosander. The banks are fringed with alder and crack willow and the water shelves deeply into the chalky green depths, as pure and clean as you could want. If it wasn't for the drone of the M25, and the Heathrow flight path, this could be the West London Lake District.

London and suburbs

41 Hampstead Ponds

Town: Hampstead
Grid ref: TQ 273862
Postcode: NW3 2SN (200m NW)

Water quality: B
Depth/size: dive, swim

Walking: 15 mins, easy
Train: Hampstead Heath, 1km
Extras: Hampstead village and the Heath

ⓘ Swimming ponds in middle of wild, hilly heath. Woody, sheltered aspect, open on one side. Changing areas and lifeguards. Green and deep. Close to train and tube.

▸ From Hampstead tube R down High St 500m, L down Downshire Hill. Cross onto Heath, 200m, bear L, to pass first then second (non-swimming) ponds. Drop down to causeway, cross pond and turn L to find entrance (£2). Ladies' and Men's ponds 1km on opposite side of Heath (Millfield Lane, Highgate West Hill, N6 6JB). www.cityoflondon.gov. uk. Swimming also on south side of Serpentine in Kensington Park (TQ 272800, SW7 1LR).

42 Eynsford, Darent

Town: Eynsford
Grid ref: TQ 539655
Postcode: DA4 0AE

Water quality: A
Depth/size: paddle, swim

Walking: 5 mins, easy
Train: Eynsford, 1km
Extras: Roman Villa and castle

ⓘ Clear, clean, shallow ford and stream beds at Eynsford (0.5m) though beware of cars. Upstream a pretty stretch of chalk stream running from Lullingstone Castle lake (murky but clean swim above small weir) and Roman Villa.

▸ From M25 J3 take exit A20 E, dir Wrotham. After 2km, at Farningham, take R, A225 dir Otford. Eynsford village and ford is on R after 1km, very popular with younger children. Follow lane and river upstream 1km to Roman Villa, then 1km to Lullingstone Castle and lake. Deeper section of river above weir as river enters lake by castle.

43 Hythe End gravel pits

Town: Staines
Grid ref: TQ 018727
Postcode: TW19 6HN (100 E)

Water quality: B
Depth/size: dive, swim

Walking: 10 mins, moderate
Train: Staines, 2km
Extras: Runnymede and Windsor

ⓘ 2km long lake one side, Colne river the other. Former gravel pit. Deep water from wooded banks. Drone of motorway and flightpath.

▸ From J13 of M25 take B376 dir Wraysbury. At first roundabout (300m) continue straight over for 150m to bridge over river Colne (but take first exit into residential side street and park and walk). Just before bridge, and by car lot, follow path onto green to find path that runs between river (L) and lake (R). This continues for 1km and is lined with willow and alder dropping into deep, gravel-bedded waters. Lake access also from S of Horton (TQ 011755).

Oxford and the Lower Thames

The Thames, from Oxford downstream, has inspired generations of charming tales from *Alice in Wonderland* to *Wind in the Willows*. Meandering through rolling countryside and stone villages, these are some of the most civilised swims in England and in many places the river is as unspoilt as it was 100 years ago, and a whole lot cleaner.

The Thames enters Oxford along Port Meadow, England's largest and oldest continuous meadow; recorded in the Doomsday Book of 1086. It has never been ploughed, and is older than any building in Oxford.

At the northern end near Wolvercote there is swimming under the bridge and beneath the weir with grand views of the dreaming spires. This is the setting and inspiration for the opening lines of *Alice in Wonderland* who was 'beginning to get very tired of sitting with her sister on the bank…' and the closing lines where Alice sees 'an ancient city and a quiet river winding near it along the plain.' At the southern end of the Meadows, closer to the train station, the river has cut out little shallow beaches along its course, popular with families. In early summer it is awash with daisies and by evening you'll see flocks of lapwing and plover rising into the sky.

Oxford has long been a wild-swimming university and the dons established a naked bathing site on the Cherwell in 1852. Christened

△ **45**

△ **46**

△ **45**

'…we all talked as if we were going to have a long swim every morning. George said it was so pleasant to wake up in the boat in the fresh morning, and plunge into the limpid river. Harris said there was nothing like a swim before breakfast to give you an appetite…'
Three Men in a Boat, 1906

the 'Parsons' Pleasure' one story tells how a number of dons were sunbathing on the banks when a group of students floated by in a punt. The startled dons covered their modesty, all except one who placed a flannel over his head explaining: 'My students know me by my face.' A site just downstream for female dons – 'Dames' Delight' – followed in 1934 but both were eventually closed in 1991. All that now remains of Parsons' Pleasure is a beer named in its honour.

Towards the end of the nineteenth century the river downstream of Oxford had already become a playground for London society. Clifton Hampden, six miles south, was a favourite with Jerome K. Jerome for boating trips. 'Sometimes we would fix up a trip of three or four days or a week, doing the thing in style and camping out.' In 1888 he wrote *Three Men in a Boat,* which became a manifesto for a simpler way of living with nature – river swimming before breakfast, kippers after and a snooze before lunch. Today the long grass and river banks are set against billowing hay fields and the area is a wonderful piece of bucolic tranquillity close to London.

Below Reading the river is still clean enough for swimming. The stretch between Hurley and Marlow is the inspiration for much of Kenneth Grahame's *Wind in the Willows*. This is where Ratty spent so much time swimming with the ducks, and Mole so much time trying not to fall in. Kenneth Graham's own childhood was spent with his grandparents being rowed out to little islands and other riverside haunts near Cookham Dean – Toad's dungeon is based on the Ice House in Bisham woods and Badger's Wildwoods is based on the Quarry Woods nearby.

Graham moved to live by the Thames after his retirement from the City in 1908. He was probably the most unlikely – and most unhappy – moneyman ever appointed to the post of secretary of the Bank of England. But within months of his early retirement he had written *Wind in the Willows*. 'As a contribution to natural history, the work is negligible,' the *Times* wrote stiffly. But Graham's fable has become one of the best-loved works in literature.

Oxford and the Lower Thames

44 Port Meadow, Thames

Town: Oxford
Grid ref: SP 488094
Postcode: OX2 8PU

Water quality: B
Depth/size: paddle, swim

Walking: 5 mins, easy
Train: Oxford, 6km
Extras: Trout Inn and The Perch pub

ⓘ 2km of river with little beaches (R bank) and grassy expanses of meadow (L bank). Shelving to up to 2m deep. Beware of boats.

▶ For north end exit to Wolvercote from A40/Woodstock Road (A4144) roundabout. Find car park 1km on L near the Trout Inn (01865 302071). For south end, turn R out of Oxford station onto main road and after 300m drop down to Thames footpath on R. Follow for 1km upstream. First footbridge leads to L bank (open meadow), next leads to R (with access to The Perch, www.the-perch. co.uk). Site of Parsons' Pleasure on Cherwell is at SP 521071.

45 Clifton Hampden, Thames

Town: Didcot
Grid ref: SU 549955
Postcode: OX14 3EF (200m E)

Water quality: B
Depth/size: paddle, swim

Walking: 10 mins, easy
Train: Culham, 2km
Extras: Barley Mow pub, camping

ⓘ A pretty bridge and pub featured in Jerome K. Jerome *Three Men in a Boat*. Sandy bays shelving to deeper water on far bank. Very long swim possible. Backdrop of wild empty meadows. Beware of boats.

▶ Village is just off A415 between Abingdon and Wallingford. Cross bridge and park opposite Barley Mow (01865 407847) and campsite. Walk back to bridge, turn R and drop down to river. River continues through fields for 2km to Dorchester and Little Wittenham (SU 568935) where good swimming is also possible below the footbridge.

46 Hurley Island, Thames

Town: Marlow
Grid ref: SU 819842
Postcode: SL6 5NB (500m W)

Water quality: B
Depth/size: paddle, swim

Walking: 15 mins, easy
Train: Marlow, 5km
Extras: Ye Old Bell (01628 825881)

ⓘ An historic village with river parkland, wooded river islands and a 1000-year-old pub. Several places to swim. Can be a bit silty plus upstream bordered by caravan park/campsite.

▶ From A/M404 between M3 and M4 take A4130 dir Henley. After 1.5km turn R to 'Hurley village only'. Park at road end in village (1km). Follow footpath from back of car park down alley to river (500m). Either: turn L and find your own place for up to 1km, or cross bridge, turn R to lock. At far end of island find shallows that lead to deeper waters (SU 829844).

△ **49** Weir Pool at Buscot Lock, Thames near Lechlade

Oxfordshire and the Upper Thames

The young Thames is a quiet river, rising in the Cotswolds and flowing peacefully through the Oxfordshire plains. Distant church spires peek over billowing wheat fields and wild flowers wave in the hedgerows. As you unzip your tent this sweet fresh river just beckons you in for an early morning swim.

Three hundred years ago things were a little busier on the upper reaches of the Thames. Lechlade was a bustling port, loading Cotswold stone and Gloucester cheese, and the new Thames and Severn Canal had just opened where the Round House now stands. But with the decline of the canals more recreational pursuits took over: Lechlade became renowned for its water carnivals and swimming galas. The ha'penny bridge, built famously high to accommodate eighteenth-century sailing barges, was popular for diving competitions. Though the organised activities have now gone, boys still jump from the bridge and the area is still a designated Waterside Park providing swimming and boating for hundreds on hot summer weekends.

The open fields of the Waterside Park are a pleasant and convenient place to swim but downstream, around Buscot and Kelmscot, the real beauty and charm of the Upper Thames begins. At the Cheese Wharf in Buscot, once a loading bay for twenty tonnes of cheese a day, there is a rope swing and deep pool for swimming and diving. Here we launched our inflatable canoe, with tent and provisions, and prepared to explore downstream.

A mile or so on, past the graceful riverside gardens of the Old Parsonage and church, the old weir at Buscot has scooped out a deep and clear natural pool, lined with weeping willow. Swimmers

△ **49** Buscot Weir Pool, River Thames

△ 47

△ 50

△ 50

splash about among the tendrils, appearing through the leaves that brush the water. The older children climb the low boughs and use them as platforms to jump in from while the younger ones play among the deep roots and use them as handrails to pull themselves out. This is a justifiably popular place for swimming. The National Trust lawns that border it are dotted with inflatable boats and deckchairs and the lock keeper is tolerant as long as you stay away from the weir itself.

Further downstream we discovered the honey-stone village of Kelmscot, once home of William Morris, the founder of the Arts and Crafts movement. Some more miles further, as evening was approaching, we put up for the night in among some tall grasses near Radcot. In these remote backwaters there are several places where discreet wild camping is acceptable if you are canoeing and arriving late. Several of the lock 'islands' – usually some miles from any road – also welcome campers who travel by foot, canoe or bicycle, but you must book. As darkness came we strung up our hammocks and watched a full moon rise through the reeds. Then, at around eleven o'clock, when the moon was high, we slipped into the water. The river was silent now, the last canal boats had long passed and the swans were sleeping in the reeds. There was just the soft sound of the water trickling as we broke the pool of silver light.

It was at least eight o'clock the next morning when we arose. Dew had covered everything but was burning off quickly. We struck camp, loaded the canoes and covered several pre-breakfast miles, arriving at Rushey Lock weir pool for a wash and the Trout Inn at Tadpole Bridge for toast and tea. Soon bulrushes towered overhead like wheat in a children's cornfield and the wild flowers of Chimney Meadows, populated by wild grasses since Saxon times, broke through; meadow barley, buttercup, crested dog's tail, lady's bedstraw and bird's-foot trefoil. Here we swam and dozed in the midday sun with the meadow pipit nesting near us among the grassy tussocks and the hares hiding their young leverets in hollows.

Oxfordshire and the Upper Thames

47 Lechlade, Thames

Town: Lechlade
Grid ref: SU 205989
Postcode: GL7 3EE

Water quality: B
Depth/size: swim, dive

Walking: 15 mins, easy
Train: Swindon, 15km
Extras: Boat trips

ⓘ A popular stretch of Thames upstream from town with good access and a junction pool for swimming. Silty shallows shelving to 2–3m. Watch kids jump from the ha'penny bridge.

◉ The Riverside Park car park is on the A361 (Swindon road) 500m south of the town bridge. Walk through fields, bearing L upriver. The most popular place to swim is in the deep shelving pool at junction with the river Coln. This is 700m upstream, above the footbridge (from which kids jump) and opposite the Roundhouse (old entrance to Thames and Severn canal, now a private dwelling). Shallow on corner shelving to 3m.

48 Cheese Wharf

Town: Lechlade
Grid ref: SU 225984 **PC:** SN7 8DA
Walking: 3 mins, easy

ⓘ Cheese Wharf is a roadside glade, deep pool in river bend, rope swing, possible to dive in from bank.

◉ From Lechlade follow A417 dir Faringdon. After 1.5km see NT Cheese Wharf sign on L with parking.

49 Buscot Weir

Town: Lechlade
Grid ref: SU 230981 **PC:** SN7 8DA
Walking: 3 mins, easy

ⓘ Buscot weir pool is large deep pool with tree swings and lawns.

◉ From Cheese Wharf continue 1km further to make sharp L turn (by mirror) and find NT car park after 300m (Buscot Weir). Continue on foot 300m to lawn on R in front of weir pool. 2km downstream to lovely pub, the Plough at Kelmscot (www.ploughkelmscot.co.uk).

50 Chimney Meadows

Town: Southmoor
Grid ref: SP 370002
Postcode: SN7 8SQ

Water quality: B
Depth/size: swim, dive, paddle

Walking: 15 mins, moderate
Train: Oxford, 17km
Extras: Tadpole Bridge hotel and pub

ⓘ Chimney Meadows nature reserve has a shallow, shady, magical woodland glade. Rushey Lock weir pool is also nearby, the other side of the Tadpole Bridge.

◉ Tadpole Bridge and the Trout Inn (01367 870382) is on Bampton–Buckland road north of A420. Turn R out of Inn, first R (400m), then R at T junction (2km), continue to road end and park on grass by nature reserve sign. Cross the bridge, over fields 1km to stream to find warm, shallow, shady ford/pool by pillbox. Follow towpath 1.6km upstream from Tadpole Bridge for Rushey Lock, weir pool (SP 324000, SN7 8RF).

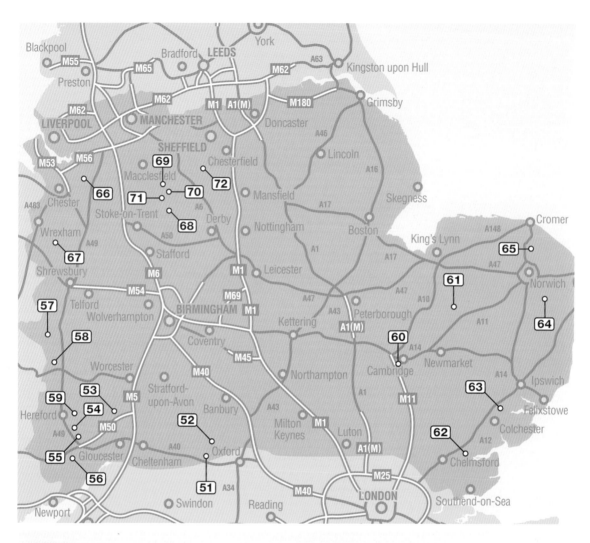

Highlights

51 Bait crayfish by the ruins of an old hall in the clear waters of the Cotswolds Windrush

52 Paddle with dinosaurs at Stonesfield, where they first found a Jurassic fossil

53 A giant amphitheatre filled with famously pure Malvern spring water. Admire tectonic faults from over 500 million years ago

54 Swim down the River Wye in Herefordshire, one of England's best-loved swimming and canoeing rivers

57 Join the famous coracle regatta at the river-swimming village of Leintwardine

60 The famous Grantchester Meadows were a popular river bathing location of Lord Byron, Rupert Brooke, Virginia Woolf and members of the Bloomsbury Group

63 Dedham Vale, an English landscape lost in time, where Constable painted *The Hay Wain* and you can still swim in the famous River Stour

64–65 Two Norfolk rivers which flow on to form the ancient Broads, great lakes cut for peat 700 years ago

68 Dove Dale is a spectacular limestone gorge with marine fossils from Britain's time spent under a shallow tropical sea

70–71 Mountain-top pools imbued with legends of mermaids and monsters

72 Setting for *Pride and Prejudice*'s Pemberley. Recreate Colin Firth's famous wild-swimming scene as the Derwent flows through the great parkland estate

Central
and East

The journey starts with the hill pools of the Malverns and the rivers of the Welsh Marches: the Wye, Teme and Lugg. In the east the alluvial soils provide warmer swims along Grantchester Meadows, the Suffolk Stour and the Norfolk Broads. Cheshire and Derbyshire provide rare meres, chalk dales and the mermaid's pools of the Peak District.

△ **51** Fishing for crayfish on the Windrush, Minster Lovell, Cotswolds

Cotswolds, Gloucestershire and Malverns

There are few counties where you can paddle with dinosaurs or swim to the centre of the earth. But in the mellow sandstone villages of the Cotswolds in Gloucestershire you can do both.

My favourite Cotswold river is the idyllic Windrush. At Bourton-on-the-Water it has ducks and high street riverways. In Little Barrington there are perfect riverside pubs and in Minster Lovell it flows past the remains of a fifteenth-century manor. Here, alongside the great old arches and ruined walls, you can bathe in the blue-tinged waters and catch crayfish big enough for supper. If you push out into the sun-dappled current you will gently bob downstream. When I was there the mayflies danced around me and fronds of water buttercup tickled my toes. A squadron of shadowy minnows darted past while some late swallows swooped low overhead.

The Evenlode is another beautiful river which runs parallel a little way to the north. It was at Stonesfield, famous for its honey-coloured stone quarries, that the first ever dinosaur remains were found in 1824. The Jurassic limestone dates back 160 million years to the time of the Megalosaurus, or the 'Great Lizard of Stonesfield', whose discovery changed the face of history. Dinosaur bones had, in fact, been found prior to the 1800s, but were thought to be the

△ **51** American Signal Crayfish

△ **53**

△ **53**

fossilised remains of some giant human, now extinct, or the bones of elephants brought to Britain by the Romans. The river here is only shallow but the vale through which it runs is beautiful, with sunny steep banks, a footbridge, pool and the remains of a Roman villa too. If you're lucky and search the riverbed you may even find your own dinosaur bones.

If you want to swim among really old rocks, though, head to the Malvern Hills in western Gloucestershire. Formed from some of the most ancient rocks on the planet more than 600 million years ago, they rise suddenly and steeply from the Severn plains affording views out of proportion to their modest height. The curative powers of the Malvern spring waters are some of the best known in the world: Tennyson came here after a nervous breakdown, Florence Nightingale stayed in 1897 and Charles Darwin visited three times. The waters were first bottled over 150 years ago and have been drunk by the royal family for more than a century. If you want to drink the water there are over 70 drinking fountains dotted across the hills, but if you want to swim in it there is only Gullet Quarry.

This old stone quarry opened in 1818 as a source of stone for Malvern town. The cliffs and crevices that surround it have quickly returned to nature in the thirty years since it closed, and the famous spring waters have filled it to create an aquamarine amphitheatre over 100 metres wide.

This is a deep and wild place. I felt like I was journeying to the centre of the earth as I swam under the tectonic folds and curling faults laid down during the earth's early formation. Buzzards circled high above, alighting on the cliff-top trees and – as I pondered the eons of time and great subterranean forces condensed in the tiny crucible around me – I felt rather small and insignificant.

Cotswolds, Gloucestershire and Malverns

51 Minster Lovell, Windrush

Town: Witney
Grid ref: SP 324113
Postcode: OX8 5RR

Water quality: A
Depth/size: paddle, swim

Walking: 5 mins, easy
Train: Finstock, 8km
Extras: Minster Lovell riverside ruins

ⓘ A small, clear, pretty Cotswold river running through the romantic grounds of the ruins. Just deep enough to swim (1m) with deeper section above weir and footbridge in meadows beyond dovecote.

▶ From A40, roundabout west of Witney, take B4047 dir Minster Lovell. After 2.5km turn L, drop down hill, over bridge and take first R, by pub. Follow lane 500m and park. Walk down through church to ruins and river. Find dovecote in adjacent field and follow river path through meadow to footbridge and weir pool. There's also access to Windrush up- and down-stream at Asthall (SP 289116).

52 Stonesfield, Evenlode

Town: Woodstock
Grid ref: SP 393165
Postcode: OX8 8PR

Water quality: A
Depth/size: paddle

Walking: 15 mins, moderate
Train: Finstock, 3km
Extras: Roman villa, dinosaurs

ⓘ Pretty footbridge and clear, clean, shallow river on grassy banks below gentle Cotswold escarpment. Does not deepen to more than 80cm. This is the sight of the first ever dinosaur find. Hunt for fossils and also examine the old Roman villa.

▶ From A40/Oxford follow A44 N, dir Witney, turn L (A4095) after 6km. After another 6km (1.5km after Long Hanborough) turn R, dir East End. After 1.5km turn R up track to Roman villa. From villa continue 200m to cross railway and after a further 200m take footpath L down to river and bridge. Shallows upstream, slightly deeper downstream.

53 Gullet Quarry

Town: Tewkesbury
Grid ref: SO 762381
Postcode: HR8 1EU (300m NW)

Water quality: A
Depth/size: swim, dive

Walking: 10mins, easy
Train: Ledbury, 6km
Extras: Malvern springs walk

ⓘ Deep, green, spring-fed quarry lake in great natural amphitheatre in cleft of Malvern hills. View millions of years of geology with birdlife circling above. Shelving entrance, sunny in the afternoon. Danger signs abound (the water is deep) so take care and don't swim alone.

▶ From Tewkesbury follow A438 dir Ledbury. After 13km, on entering Hollybush, turn R. After 1km bear R and park. Walk up dead-end lane on L to quarry (300m). Enter quarry lake by slipway on far R. Also accessible 4km from J2 of M50. For spring locations see www.thespasdirectory.com.

△ **55** Near Backney Common on the River Wye

Lower Wye and Herefordshire

I spent my early childhood close to the Herefordshire Wye, near Hoarwithy. We were two families and a gang of five children. I was the youngest and would trail along behind as rafts were built and lanes explored by bicycle. It's easy to be nostalgic about a river when it flows through the heart of your formative years.

When I tried to remember some of the places I had swum on the Wye, however, I realised many were lost in the fog of early memories, so I decided to return to Hoarwithy for a week and retrace old steps.

I based myself at Tressacks campsite, a plain but pleasant stretch of riverside with a little beach, roaring campfires and an excellent gastro pub. Each morning I tiptoed sleepily down to the river and plunged groggily into the shallow waters and was brought to life with a judder of adrenalin. I had played near here as a young boy, I thought, though the river seemed so much wider and deeper then. On really big expeditions we would cycle the three miles to Sellack Common and it used to take all day. The height of excitement was standing on the white iron suspension footbridge, bouncing up and down to see if it would swing and dropping blackcurrants on canoes as they went by.

The Wye is lucky to be one of the several rivers in England with an Act of Parliament that enshrines the right to navigate, and to swim. Some suggest that all rivers navigable by small craft have automatic rights of navigation but even here on the Wye, one of the most famous canoeing rivers, there are still occasional conflicts between fishermen and other river users.

△55

△56

△ **54** Tressacks campsite, Hoarwithy

From Sellack Common the river completes a five-mile loop to Backney through mainly private fishing estates, but a mile-long lane, over the brow of a hill, cuts off the corner and brings you to Backney Common. This area of meadow has age-old commoner rights and occupies the inside of a large, deep meander. A wide pebble beach has been deposited over time on the inside bank and large deep swimming holes have been eroded on the outside. The sand and pebbles are beautifully graded so you can even bring your bucket and spade.

Some seven miles downstream the river comes to its most splendid reach as it enters the great wooded ravine of Symonds Yat. Beech-forested cliffs climb up on all sides and King Arthur's and Merlin's Caves can be spied high on the limestone walls, cut by the river many thousands of years ago. The village is squeezed onto the narrow rising banks of the gorge and the east and west side are joined only by two rope ferries. It is possible to swim across but most inhabitants use canoes. Many homes – and even the church – have river landing stages which double up for river swimming in the summer. The village is equally famous as a place for learning about rivers and the great outdoors: the Biblins forest camp in Symonds Yat has been giving inner city children wild experiences for over 50 years.

The Wye is the most popular canoeing river in Britain and many companies will arrange everything needed for a few days canoe-camping through the countryside. There is also the beautiful Wye Valley Walk and it was at Symonds Yat that I met an elderly couple from Lincoln who had walked for over thirty miles, swimming along the way. They had come rather unstuck skinny-dipping one lunchtime just as a flotilla of canoes helmed by a stag party in fancy dress came by! Despite that, they had a strict routine of swimming three times a day: 'Before breakfast, lunch and tea we agreed – its very good for you, you know, going in the cold water. And we haven't missed an opportunity yet.'

Lower Wye and Herefordshire

54 Sellack Bridge

Town: Ross-on-Wye
Grid ref: SO 566280
Postcode: HR9 6LT (300m N)

Water quality: A
Depth/size: paddle, swim

Walking: 15 mins, moderate
Train: Hereford, 15km
Extras: Tressacks campsite and pub

ℹ Beautiful open common by small church with shingle beach shelving to deep section (2m) on far bank. Elegant white suspension footbridge. Fishermen also fish here and will say it's dangerous! Poor parking so cycle, walk or canoe.

▶ From Ross, take A49 dir Hereford. After roundabout with A40, take second turn on R after 700m, dir Hoarwithy. After 3km, at telephone box at Pict's Cross, turn R into narrow lane then, 1.2km on L, turn down to Sellack church, 600m. Basic campsite at Tressacks (open fires and riverside, 01432 840235) in Hoarwithy, 3km, behind excellent New Harp Inn. (www.newharpinn.co.uk, 01432 840900).

55 Backney Common

Town: Ross-on-Wye
Grid ref: SO 588269
Postcode: HR9 6QX (500m SE)

Water quality: A
Depth/size: paddle, swim

Walking: 15 mins, moderate
Train: Hereford, 18km
Extras: Near site of old railway

ℹ Ancient but little known common in tight loop of Wye providing large shingle and sandy beach shelving to large deep pool. Undisputed access. Large swan population, with droppings.

▶ From Ross, take A49 dir Hereford. After roundabout with A40, take first turn on R, 300m, dir Foy/Backney. After 3km, at T-junction, turn R and 200m on R find parking and picnic site. Exit car park to lane and immediately on sharp R follow shady trackway 200m, through 2 gates, find large field (the common). River on both sides but head to far end for beach and pool (500m).

56 Symonds Yat

Town: Ross-on-Wye
Grid ref: SO 559167
Postcode: HR9 6BW (300m E)

Water quality: A
Depth/size: paddle, swim, dive

Walking: 5 mins, moderate
Train: Lydney, 14km
Extras: Ye Olde Ferrie Inne and ferry

ℹ Small sandy bay, meadows, shelving to 2m. Large rocks on far bank.

▶ 5km N of Monmouth on A40 (dir Ross) exit just after services. Follow signs to Symonds Yat West. Follow road 1.5km into village and bear L down steep lane, 100m after Paddocks Hotel, to Ye Olde Ferrie Inn (01600 890 232). Walk upstream 300m to find grassland and small beach down steep bank on R. Note large boulders on opposite bank, also popular for swims, accessible from Symonds Yat East. Also 2km downstream, past rapids, lovely woods and more remote swims in the stretch to 'The Biblins' (SO 552144).

△ **58** Weir pools on the Teme

Welsh Marches: Teme, Lugg and Arrow

The Teme – part Welsh, part English – means the 'dark one' in ancient Celtic and is one of several rivers that drain the Welsh Marches. It is wild and beautiful and is locally known for its annual coracle regatta at Leintwardine.

Coracles are one of the oldest boat designs in Britain, and were used by bronze-age Britons and invading Romans alike. They are oval in shape, rather like half a walnut shell, and traditionally made from interwoven willow rods tied with willow bark, covered in horse or bullock hide and sealed with a thin layer of tar. Designed for use in swiftly flowing shallow streams, such as those on the Welsh border rivers, they don't have a keel and only need a few inches in which to float. This makes them very light – perfect if you're a poacher and need to flee – and very manoeuvrable.

It's just as well that the Teme at Leintwardine is an excellent swimming river because the coracle's manoeuvrability makes it inherently unstable – spinning round on the spot and all too easily tipping you in. If you haven't yet honed the necessary skills, the Leintwardine coracle regatta is the perfect place to combine some training with plenty of opportunity for an involuntary river dip.

The village's main swimming stretch runs from the road bridge upriver past the rope swing to a largish pool where the River Clun joins the Teme. With gardens running right down to the river, these backs have a rather civilised and homely feel. A little further on the

△ 59

△ 58

*'Upon the glittering
stream behold,*

*Those fishermen,
of courage bold,*

*In numerous pairs,
pursue their trade,*

*In coracles,
themselves have made;*

*Formed of slight twigs
with flannel cas'd,*

*O'er which three coats
of tar are plac'd.*

And (as a porter bears his pack)

*Each mounts his vessel
on his back.'*

With reference to
the River Teme, 1794

meadow opens out and the river runs fast over wide pebble rills with some deeper holes and lively currents.

The Teme, which eventually joins the Severn, is just one of the many rivers that drain down from the Radnorshire hills and form this historic stretch of the Welsh 'Marches', a borderland of battle grounds and fiefdoms that the Normans attempted to control from 1066 onwards. The River Lugg runs parallel a few miles to the south and eventually joins the Wye. At its valley head stands the church of Pilleth, meaning 'the pool on the hill'. In 1402 it was the site for one of the bloodiest and most important battles in a thousand years of Welsh independence wars. Despite the great massacre here, and the burning of the church, its holy well is still revered for its healing powers. Tadpoles and great crested newts also seem to thrive in its shallow waters.

It was not until we'd travelled another twelve miles downstream of Pilleth, way past Presteigne, that a friend and I actually found somewhere for a proper swim in the Lugg. Just outside Leominster near the village of Eyton, in a perfect rural landscape, you'll find several weirs and river pools. The Arrow runs close by and we started searching for a shallow ford that was the location of an idyllic toddlers' picnic party he had attended thirty years before and which he wanted to relocate. We found the site, homing in using a photo as a guide, and a mile upstream discovered a long weir pool, which provided a deeper swim in dark, peaty water through a tree-lined avenue of emerald alders.

The Arrow eventually joins the Lugg downstream of Leominister and we stopped for an afternoon dip at Hope under Dinmore before continuing on some miles to Lugg Meadows near Hereford. These are the largest known modern example of 'Lammas' meadows in Britain, with ownership divided into strips marked by dole stones. The meadows are still managed in accordance with this medieval system and an active commoners' association controls the grazing rights. With its intermittent gravel beaches and deeper pools we part swum, part waded the length of the Lugg that evening, floating in the low light past banks awash with cow parsley and meadow shank.

Welsh Marches: Teme, Lugg and Arrow

57 Leintwardine, Teme

Town: Ludlow
Grid ref: SO 403738
Postcode: SY7 0LA (50m S)

Water quality: A
Depth/size: paddle, swim, current

Walking: 5 mins, easy
Train: Ludlow, 11km
Extras: Coracle regatta and pub

ⓘ A stretch of open common with pub, bridge, church and rope swings. Deepish junction pool. Little beaches and fun currents upstream.

◗ Leintwardine is 14km west of Ludlow on the A49 then A4113. Park near bridge or at Lion Hotel. Walk upstream 50m to rope swing. 100m beyond this find the River Clun junction pool with shelving beach. 200m further on are pebble shallows interspersed with deep holes. For a pretty downstream river walk: cross to lane opposite pub and turn R onto footpath after 400m. Or follow lane by side of pub (next to garage) 300m upstream to footbridge on Clun.

58 Eyton, Lugg and Arrow

Town: Leominster
Grid ref: SO 468609
Postcode: HR6 0AQ (500m SW)

Water quality: A
Depth/size: swim, paddle

Walking: 15 mins, moderate
Train: Leominster, 3km/16km
Extras: Pilleth church, near Presteigne

ⓘ Teme runs through sunny open fields, often shallow but with deep pools above several weirs.

◗ 1km N of Leominster on B4361 turn L down lane dir Eyton. Turn L after 1km and find footpath L after 500m. Walk to bottom R of field, 400m, and enter water meadows. Walk upstream 300m to find footbridge. Follow footpath downstream 1km to weir pool. Weir pool upstream too. Further (dark and shady) weir pool 14km west on Arrow at Staunton-on-Arrow. From Staunton village church turn L then L at T junction for 1km until footpath sign L. Follow path 80m (SO 361603).

59 Lugg Meadows

Town: Hereford
Grid ref: SO 530414
Postcode: HR1 1JD (500m E)

Water quality: A
Depth/size: swim, paddle, current

Walking: 10 mins, easy
Train: Hereford, 2km
Extras: Hereford city cathedral

ⓘ Large meadows just outside Hereford. Meandering gentle river with deep holes (2m) in bends and plenty of shelving gravel beaches.

◗ Long swim also possible the length of meadow (2km) from A4103 to A438. Follow A465 2km from city centre (dir Bromyard), up Aylestone Hill, past college (on R), down hill then turn R up Walney Lane (opp. Overbury Rd). Park and walk on into the meadows to river 500m. Good deep pools in bends up- or downstream. Also try Lugg upstream, N of Hereford, behind Bodenham Church (SO 530509). Turn R off A49 12km N of Hereford (2km before Hope-on-Dinmore).

△ **60** The River Cam along Grantchester Meadows

Cambridge and East Anglia

Take tea at Grantchester and enjoy a stretch of river and meadows that is little changed since Edwardian times.

Grantchester was already a fashionable location for Cambridge students when the boyish, charismatic, 22-year-old graduate Rupert Brooke became a resident in 1909, commuting to and from Cambridge in his canoe and often 'sitting in the midst of admiring females with nothing on but an embroidered sweater'. In Cambridge it was an age of relaxed elegance: long walking tours, sleeping under canvas, picnicking on the grass and naked bathing. Many brilliant young minds gathered around Brooke and his outdoor lifestyle.

Today it seems little has changed along Grantchester Meadows. On a hot summer day the languid mile-long stretch of river is dotted with leisurely picnic parties. Punts and canoes glide by, some heading downstream towards Cambridge's famous 'Backs', others heading upstream to the tea gardens in Grantchester village. At intervals you hear another splash as either a punter or picnicker decides to cool off.

Paradise Pool is a narrow wooded area on the edge of town at the top end of the Meadows. There's a curly tree ideal for diving but anywhere along the Meadows is good for swimming, particularly on the outside of the bends where the river deepens, often to over six foot. Be warned though: while the river is clear, clean and warm, the banks and bed are muddy and squelchy.

△ **62** Ulting Church, River Chelmer

△ **60** Paradise Pool

△ **60** The Orchard Tea Gardens

'In Grantchester their skins are white;

They bathe by day, they bathe by night;'

From *The Old Vicarage, Grantchester*
Rupert Brooke, 1912

Many of East Anglia's rivers suffer from siltation and high quantities of fertiliser run-off, a side effect of the alluvial soils and intensive agriculture in the region. The Cam is actually one of the cleanest rivers in the area, though you should never swim in the actual city or along the 'Backs' where the sewers can harbour rats and Weil's disease. The Chelmer river in East Essex, in part converted to navigation, is also a very clean river and there is no more charming place than by the riverside church at Ulting. For the very clearest waters in East Anglia, though, head for the chalk lands of Thetford Forest and Santon Downham, 20 miles to the north of Cambridge.

Back on the Cam, Grantchester village is a good place to end your explorations. The Orchards has served tea from its meandering gardens for well over a hundred years. A great lounging sweep of meadow reaches down to the water's edge and the deckchairs and low wicker tables are a wonderful place to refuel after a long punt or swim.

It was here that Brooke and the young Bloomsbury Group spent long summers camping and river bathing. Virginia Woolf, who once went naked night-swimming with Brooke near here, christened her Grantchester friends the 'Neo-Pagans'. Their philosophy was for a simpler, gentler lifestyle, closer and more in tune with nature with strong values of reciprocity and friendship.

These idyllic times in Cambridge were to be short-lived. Rupert Brooke died tragically just a few years later in the First World War, aged 28. He was widely recognised posthumously for his poetry, including 'The Soldier' and became a symbol of the innocence of youth and the appreciation of simple pleasures and pastimes. When his contemporary Bertrand Russell returned to Grantchester after the war he said of Brooke's death: 'I am feeling the weight of the war much more since I came back here…with all the usual Grantchester life stopped. There will be other generations – yet I keep fearing that something of civilisation will be lost for good…' Visit Grantchester, punt and swim, and ensure Brooke's legacy lives on.

Cambridge and East Anglia

60 Grantchester Meadows

Town: Cambridge
Grid ref: TL 445571
Postcode: CB3 9JJ (100m S)

Water quality: B
Depth/size: dive, swim

Walking: 5 mins, easy
Train: Cambridge 1.8km
Extras: The Orchard Tea Garden

ℹ A range of swimming opportunities along 2km of the meadows ending at the Orchard Tea Garden. Deep banks make this good for diving, but it can be muddy! Some weeds but clean. Upstream of the city.

▷ From M11 J12 enter city by A603, becoming Newnham Road. 2.5km, as road bends to L, turn R down Newnham Street (residential) becoming Grantchester Meadows at bend. At bend find footpath L, heading to river and fallen tree 200m, Paradise Pool, or continue on to car park at the Meadows. 150m on to meadow find tight river bend and good, deep open pool.

61 Santon, Little Ouse

Town: Thetford
Grid ref: TL 826873
Postcode: IP27 0TT (200m W)

Water quality: B
Depth/size: paddle, swim

Walking: 1 min, easy
Train: Thetford/Brandon 5km
Extras: Thetford Forest walks

ℹ 30km further up the A11 from Cambridge. Pretty chalk stream running through forest with shelving access above footbridge next to car park at end of remote lane. Chalky riverbed, up to 2m deep, long swim possible.

▷ From A11 Thetford roundabout take B1107 dir Brandon. After 4km turn R dir Santon Down. 1.7km, in Santon Down village, bear R, over bridge and take first R. Park in car park (1km) before church and road end. River and footbridge immediately below. Or, from Santon Downham, park next to village hall and find small path to river and landing platform just below bridge.

62 Ulting Church, Chelmer

Town: Hatfield Peverel
Grid ref: TL 801088
Postcode: CM9 6QU (100m S)

Water quality: B
Depth/size: swim, dive

Walking: 1 min, easy
Train: Hatfield Peverel 3km
Extras: Riverside church

ℹ A secluded little church on the banks of the river Chelmer where people sunbathe and sometimes swim. Wide, deep section used by pleasure crafts and slightly brown, but water is some of the cleanest of any Essex river. 2m deep.

▷ Follow A12 7km NE of Chelmsford and exit at Hatfield Peverel. Turn L then first R onto B1019 dir Maldon. 600m, still in village, turn off on R fork, dir Utling and Woodham Walter. Ulting church is down gravel track on R by telephone box after 2.2km. Park and walk to back of church to find river, and probably canal boats moored.

△ **64** Outney Common on the Waveney

Suffolk and Norfolk

Two hundred years after Constable painted it, Willy Lott's cottage still sits pretty by the banks of the pastoral Stour, the spire of Dedham church rising above the meadows as ever and the wide majestic sky is filled with purple-tinged clouds.

The horse-drawn hay wain may no longer trundle across the river's millstream at Flatford, but there is still something of antiquity and calm in this little vale. As a boy, John Constable spent his childhood fishing, swimming and exploring, the soft light and wide skies inspiring him to become a painter. 'I may yet make some impression,' he wrote, 'with my "light", my "dews", my "breezes" – my bloom and my freshness – no one of which qualities has yet been perfected on the canvas of any painter in the world.'

From Dedham village it's a mile's meander down to Flatford Mill via Fen Bridge. I was to meet a friend, Rosy, and her little girl. They have swum in the pool beneath the bridge all their lives.

Further downstream, on our way to find chocolate cake and tea at Flatford Mill, we swam again. The distinctive bank-side willows, planted and pollarded over a hundred years ago, have grown into fat great sinewy bundles. The water is dark with occasional strands of weeds floating up from the bottom, but the river is warm, clear and clean.

△ 63

△ 63

△ 65

There also used to be barges on the river and, though the locks and wharfs have disappeared, the public still retain the right to navigate from Sudbury to the sea. The Stour is now a popular canoeing and boating river and you'll find many clinker rowing boats filling its reaches in summer.

As the Stour forms Suffolk's border with Essex, so the Waveney forms its border with Norfolk, while also being the southernmost of the Norfolk Broads. The Waveney was also the local river of the late Roger Deakin, modern father of wild-swimming, whose beautiful book, *Waterlog*, detailed his journey swimming through Britain by river, lake and sea. Outney Common is one of the best places to swim in the Waveney with excellent riverside access for more than a mile. Deakin paddled his canoe, Cigarette, along here as part of a Radio 4 documentary exploring the natural history of the river.

The nearby landscape of the Norfolk Broads, a unique low-lying patchwork of interlocking rivers and lakes, was originally believed to have been formed as the result of natural processes. It was not until the 1950s that Joyce Lambert proved otherwise. She showed that the sides of the deep lakes should be gently sloping if naturally formed, but instead they were steep. She also analysed the high demand for peat fuel in the middle ages, suggesting the lakes were in fact flooded peat quarries abandoned in the fourteenth century as the sea levels began to rise and inundate them.

'I associate my careless boyhood with all that lies on the banks of the Stour. Those scenes made me a painter, and I am grateful...'
John Constable to a friend, 1814

Once perfectly clean and clear, the Broads have suffered from pollution over the last thirty years with increasing algae concentration from the intensification of Norfolk farming. Now several projects are working to remove nutrients using reed bales. However, the upstream reaches are still mainly clean and the Bure, north of Buxton and Lamas, provides one of the prettiest river swimming stretches.

Suffolk and Norfolk

63 Dedham Vale

Town: Dedham
Grid ref: TM 067336
Postcode: CO7 6DY

Water quality: C
Depth/size: paddle, swim

Walking: 20 mins, moderate
Train: Manningtree, 3km
Extras: Flatford Mill (NT) and row boat hire

ⓘ A beautiful open historic vale, site of Flatford Mill, where people row on boats and occasionally swim. Fen Bridge is a quiet spot with 2m deep river pools and shelving access. Some weeds to watch for. Grade C due to fertiliser content (nitrates) but safe enough to swim.

▶ 7km N of Colchester on A12, exit dir Stratford St Mary and Dedham. Bear R then R again and continue 1km to Dedham. Walk on L bank 1.2km to Fen Bridge for pool below. Simple riverside campsite near Wissington, 13km west (TL 950334, www.riverstourboating.org.uk, 01206 262350).

64 Outney Common

Town: Bungay
Grid ref: TM 334908
Postcode: NR35 1HG (500m NE)

Water quality: B
Depth/size: swim

Walking: 15 mins, moderate
Train: Beccles, 10km
Extras: Boat and bike hire

ⓘ A 3km stretch of the Waveney meandering around open common land. Good water quality, up to 2m deep in parts, popular for canoeing. Many bays and swimming possibilities.

▶ At the first Bungay roundabout on A143 (from Diss) take first exit signed 'Outney Common Caravan Park'. This site provides canoes, camping and bikes. Follow footpath, which skirts around outer edge of the caravan park coming onto open common land and footbridge over stream (400m). Bear R 150m to find bend of river Waveney, or continue straight to next footbridge (300m) (www.outneymeadow.co.uk).

65 Lamas, River Bure

Town: Buxton
Grid ref: TG 239229
Postcode: NR10 5EJ (500m NE)

Water quality: A
Depth/size: swim

Walking: 15 mins, moderate
Train: Hoveton and Wroxham, 7km
Extras: Pleasure boat hire at Wroxham

ⓘ A quiet, rural idyllic stretch of the Bure river, flowing past gardens, fields and a church. Deep and clear running. Banks can be rather wet and marshy.

▶ Buxton mill is 15km N of Norfolk and off the A140 Cromer road. Turn R 10km N of the A1042 junction. The large white mill building is just outside Buxton on the road to Lamas. Some parking behind the mill though the footpath is on the river's R on other side, accessed via front of mill. Continue up river to bend and pool, 600m, or continue on for up to 5km to Brampton and chose a spot anywhere along the bank.

△ **68** Lathkill Dale near Dovedale, Peak District

West Midlands Meres, Mosses and Dales

The West Midlands' meres and mosses are some of the last remaining fragments of ancient peat bogs in the country. They form one of our most important habitats in Britain with new species still being discovered.

There are important lakes near Ellesmere and Colemere but Delamere – the forest of the meres – is Cheshire's most important area of wetland. The lakes were laid down 10,000 years ago at the end of the last ice age. As the melt took hold, huge iceberg-sized chunks fell away from the undersides of the glaciers and became trapped in pockets of earth and mud on the newly revealed ground. When they finally melted and collapsed they left large depressions – kettle holes – that evolved into freshwater lakes. Some were then colonised by sphagnum moss, which would entirely fill the shallows, soaking up rainwater and swelling like a sponge to many times its original size to form higher wetland areas called 'mosses'. These endangered lowland bogs have unique flora and fauna and have been drained, farmed or destroyed in many other parts of the country.

Hatchmere, nestling in the corner of Delamere, is a serene, reed-banked lagoon that has been popular with wild-swimmers for generations. A small bay leads to sandy shallows that can reach 80° fahrenheit at the height of summer. Late afternoon sun filters through the forest canopy. Dark, dappled green waters reach out ahead and jewel-blue dragonflies whirr low over the water.

△ 66

△ 67

△ 67

This area is particularly well known for dragonflies – including the White-faced Darter and the Southern Hawker – and swimming in the lake is a fantastic way to get up close without disturbing them. As you glide through the water, nose peeping up from the surface, you are just another part of the lake's ecosystem. Hatchmere has always been a popular place for families and there is little evidence to suggest that swimming in the lake has a detrimental effect on wildlife. This site, however, was the centre of a major struggle between local people, a private fishing club and the wildlife trust that bought the lake in 1998. The trust, unaware of the lake's use as a summertime swimming hole, initially gave exclusive license to the fishing club who, in turn, tried to fence out the swimmers. A huge campaign ensued with local families and media lobbying for the people's right to swim and paddle. Now fishermen occupy one end of the lake and families the other. Signs say 'swimming not advised' – to cover liability issues – but dipping in the water is lawful and popular again.

To the west another popular uprising by working people seeking access to their countryside took place over 75 years ago. On 24 April 1932 over 600 walkers from nearby cities took to the moors, then currently reserved only for grouse shooting, in the Kinder Scout Marches and mass trespass. Six were arrested but their campaign eventually led to the establishment of Britain's first ever national park – The Peak District – in 1951.

At the heart of the park Dovedale and Lathkill are truly spectacular limestone gorges. Dovedale is a mainly shallow river but there are deeper sections under the ancient rock caves and limestone cliffs of Dove Holes and Raven's Tor. At Lover's Leap a young woman, hearing that her fiancé had been killed in the Napoleonic Wars, threw herself from the cliff but was saved when her billowing dress caught in the trees. This entire area is made of old coral that used to lie at the bottom of a 350 million-year-old tropical sea. You can still find fossils of ancient crinoids or 'sea lilies' by the stepping-stones at the south end of the dale and Thorpe Cloud Hill is actually the remains of an old tropical atoll on the seabed.

West Midlands Meres, Mosses and Dales

66 Hatchmere

Town: Hatchmere
Grid ref: SJ 554722
Postcode: WA6 6NQ

Water quality: B
Depth/size: paddle, swim

Walking: 2 mins, easy
Train: Delamere, 2km
Extras: The Carrier's Inn

ⓘ A relatively shallow, warm 300m–long lake in the nationally important wildlife area of Delamere Forest. A grassy area next to the B road leads to small reed-lined bays and shallows. The lake deepens to about 3m with plenty of room for a long swim. Be respectful to fishermen.

▶ Hatchmere is located between Chester, Runcorn and Northwich, 10km S of the M56 (J12). From Frodsham continue on B5152 6km S to find lake on R, followed by The Carrier's Inn (01928 787877) 100m further. Woodland walks and bike rides: Delamere Forest Park (01606 889792). Read about its history at www.hatchmere.com.

67 Colemere and Ellesmere

Town: Ellesmere
Grid ref: SJ 436330
Postcode: SY12 0QL (500m E)

Water quality: B
Depth/size: swim

Walking: 5 mins, easy
Train: Gobowen, 13km
Extras: Ellesmere Lake

ⓘ An area of nine glacial meres. Colemere is remote, beautiful and quiet with a shore path and small sailing club. Sometimes blue–green algae is reported. Be discreet.

▶ Colemere Country Park is between Whitchurch and Shrewsbury at junction of A495 and A528, 1km south of Welshampton. The lake shore to R of sailing club, closest to car park, is sandy and shelving. Or follow the lake path to R to find other, more discreet entry points. Some also swim from Ellesmere, 3km N. Heading into town from S, lake on R, pass church and turn R up Swan Lane. Continue 800m to find footpath on R (SJ 408353).

68 Dovedale and Lathkill

Town: Thorpe
Grid ref: SK 151514
Postcode: DE6 2AY (1.2km NE)

Water quality: A
Depth/size: paddle, plunge

Walking: 20 mins, moderate
Train: Uttoxeter, 22km
Extras: Dovedale Walk

ⓘ A stunning deep limestone gorge with caves, rock spires and shallow pools. Popular stepping stones good for paddling at the S end.

▶ Cross bridge and walk 1km upstream (on river's L) to the Stepping Stones (SK 151514). Continue further 3km (one hour) through woods, passing many shallow pools, to Dove Hole, a deeper section in river with current, cliffs and caves (SK 143536). The Dove is also deep at Mapleton Bridge, 2km S of Thorpe (SK 164481). Also worth exploring: similar limestone gorge with shallow pools and weirs at Lathkill Dale, Over Haddon, near Bakewell (SK 184657).

△ **69** The second plunge pool downstream of Three Shires Head

Derbyshire and the Peaks

On Axe Edge Moor, high in the Peak District at the headwaters of the Dane, there's a riotous little creek that gushes down the hillside along narrow grassy banks before dropping into a pool beneath two medieval bridges.

This is Three Shires Head, so-named because the three counties of Derbyshire, Staffordshire and Cheshire have their boundaries on the old packhorse bridge.

The residents of nearby Flash, the highest village in the country, put this giddy political geography to good use, holding illegal boxing matches on the no-man's land of the bridge where no county sheriff could arrest them. Renowned for making counterfeit 'Flash' money they came to Three Shires Head to exchange it for goods.

The moor was deserted as I approached across the hillside, squelching through the legacy of a week of summer rains. Dark clouds had blocked out the sun again and a warm westerly wind whipped at my coat. The storms of the previous days had enlarged the mountain tub to a raging, frothy cauldron. Giant ferns were billowing about like the bendy palms of a tropical typhoon and great bubbles the size of footballs were moving in circles around the pool. Overheated and sweaty after the walk I stripped and plunged, buffeted by currents of the wild jacuzzi. A cluster of bubbles took off in a gust, floating down the valley before being caught on the gorse.

△ 70

△ 72

'A great thing rose up from the middle of the lake… 25 to 30 feet tall… and those eyes were extremely malevolent. It pointed its bony fingers menacingly at me so there was no mistaking its hostility…'

Mrs Florence Pettit on visiting Doxey Pool in 1949, just as she was about to swim.

Over at Doxey Pool they say the waters are bottomless. This tiny tarn is on top of the Roaches – a great dragon tail of rocks that marks the western boundary of the Peak District. That night, at the remote Mermaid's Inn, that looks over The Roaches from some miles away, they told me about the legend of a local beauty who was accused of witchcraft by a spurned admirer and was drowned in another nearby tarn: the Mermaid's Pool, also marked on maps as Blake Mere. Three day's later the man was also found dead in the pool, his face torn by talons. Now no animal or human will dare go there.

In Celtic times small pools and standing waters were viewed as a doorway between the terrestrial and spirit worlds. Generally these pools were seen as bringers of life and of fertility but the spirits could be unpredictable. Another Mermaid's Pool stands under Kinder Scout further north. If you see the mermaid on Easter Day she will either imbue you with eternal life or drag you under, depending on her mood.

The next morning the Mermaid's Pool by the Inn made a chilly wake-up call but I emerged unharmed. Rain clouds were rolling in from the west again as I set off in search of more recent history. There can be few more popular screen moments than when Colin Firth, playing Mr Darcy in the BBC's *Pride and Prejudice*, goes swimming in the lake at Pemberley, to emerge dripping from the waters, his shirt unbuttoned and clinging to his chest, his breeches sodden and his dark hair a tangled mess. The scene helped turn Firth into a romantic icon.

Both Lyme Hall and Chatsworth House have played Pemberley but Chatsworth's River Derwent is the more popular location for a summer swim. Landscaped by Capability Brown, the mountain river was deepened and straightened between two weirs. Soft red sands line the banks and with the light low, once the coach crowds have departed, the still waters allow for a long and most aristocratic swim.

Derbyshire and the Peaks

69 Three Shires Head, Dane

Town: Flash
Grid ref: SK 010685
Postcode: SK17 0SW (2km NW)

Water quality: A
Depth/size: plunge, paddle

Walking: 1 hour, difficult
Train: Buxton, 10km
Extras: New Inn pub, Flash

ⓘ Two waterfalls and plunge pools (shallow, 1m) plus bridges set in the small but wild valley at the headwaters of the river Dane. Famous for counterfeit money and skulduggery. High moor, good views.

▶ Flash is R off the A53 9km S of Buxton (dir Leek). Park and bear R down steep narrow lane and follow for 1.2km (20mins). At Spring Head Farm take footpath R (NW) 1km down hill to stream, up again, into Dane valley, then 1km up to bridge by Three Shire's Head. Find shallow Panniers Pool and falls under the bridges but also larger pool 200m downstream. Take map.

70 Mermaid's Pool

Town: Leek
Grid ref: SK 040613 **PC:** ST13 8UN
Walking: 1 min, moderate

ⓘ Tiny moor-top pool steeped in legend with views of The Roaches.

▶ From Leek head N on A53 for 6km. At crossroads, by telephone box and pub, turn R for Mermaid Inn moor-top pub (01538 300253). The tiny tarn is 3km on R by side of road. Another Mermaid's Pool is found 27km N, under Kinder Scout (SK 075887).

71 Doxey Pool

Town: Leek
Grid ref: SK 003629 **PC:** ST13 8UB
Walking: 40 min, difficult

ⓘ Haunted pool high on Roaches ridge top.

▶ On ridge top of the Roaches itself. About 1km from Roaches car park, 1.5km behind Upper Hulme, off A53 (4km from Leek on L).

72 Chatsworth, Derwent

Town: Baslow
Grid ref: SK 260693
Postcode: DE45 1PP (500m S)

Water quality: A
Depth/size: paddle, swim

Walking: 15 mins, moderate
Train: Chesterfield, 15km
Extras: Chatsworth House and gardens

ⓘ A graceful sweep of the river Derwent. Long river pools with fantastic Chatsworth parkland views. Red, sandy river bed and lawns for picnics. Shallows shelving to 2m deep. Be discreet.

▶ Chatsworth is on B6012, well signed from Baslow, Bakewell and beyond. Unless visiting the house, park at Calton Lees car park 1km S of house (£2). Drop down to river and walk upstream to choose a quiet place away from the house, and avoid areas close to the two large weirs. There is also a long stretch of more sheltered, secluded river and parkland north of house and bridge.

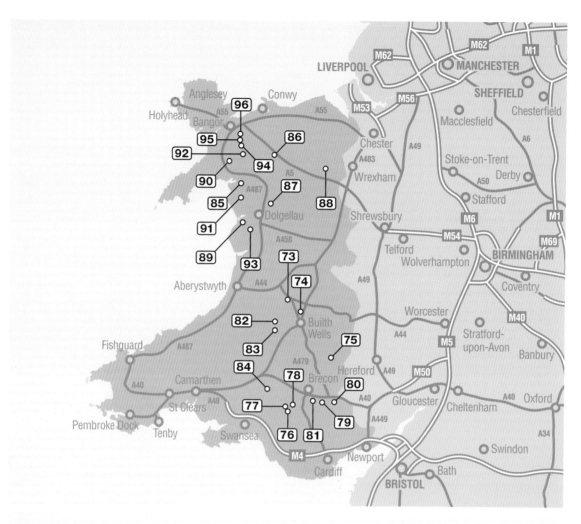

Highlights

73 The Elan Valley was home to Shelley, who loved to bathe in mountain pools and sail toy boats down the stream

75 Hay-on-Wye, home of literary festivals and second-hand bookshops, is also the site of the famous riverside 'Warren' – a stretch of Wye-side shingle and shallows popular with families

76–78 The Waterfalls Woods are the most spectacular series of waterfalls in Wales, with aqua forest lidos fit for the gods

81 A series of remote waterfalls on the side of the Brecon Beacons with stunning views

82 Wolf's Leap in the wild Cambrian Mountains was home to wolves and is now famous for red kites

84 This high tarn is haunted by King Arthur's 'Lady of the Lake'

86 Fairy Glen is one of the most beautiful gorges in the popular Betws-y-Coed tourist area

87 Waterfalls plunge through a valley rich in Welsh gold. There are several ruined mines and you can still find gold if you pan the pools

88–89 Coloured azure blue by faint traces of copper, these fantastic old slate quarries are like Mediterranean lagoons

91–93 Tarn-swimming is the ultimate landscape immersion and wilderness trip. These are three of the best

94–96 Follow in the footsteps of Mallory, Hillary and some of our most famous Everest mountaineers and complete the Snowdon swim tour

Wales

A region of waterfalls, woods, deep azure quarry pools and the famous gorges, cataracts and llyns of Snowdonia. This is a country of wild magical landscapes with rowan-clad plunge pools, mountain lakes and secret chasms in Tolkien-style profusion.

△ **74** Pen-doll Rocks, River Wye, Builth Wells

Upper Wye and Elan

The Elan Valley is sometimes known as the Welsh Lake District and was the romantic inspiration for Shelley's early years. It is also the Welsh Wye's first major stop on its journey from its source in the Cambrian Mountains towards the literary haven of Hay-on-Wye.

Percy Shelley – the idealist, revolutionary and great romantic poet – first visited his uncle's estate in the Elan when he was 18, walking there from Sussex over the course of a week. Already having a reputation as a strange but fun-filled young man, he used to bathe in the mountain streams and sail toy boats down the currents, sometimes with a cat on board. He fell in love in the valley and tried to make a life there with his first wife but when they failed to acquire a house the marriage collapsed. She drowned herself in the Serpentine in London two years later. He lost his life at sea in Italy aged 29.

The Elan stream in which Shelley used to bathe and both the valley homes he loved so much – Cwm Elan and the manor house Nangwyllt – were also drowned by a series of Victorian reservoirs in the late nineteenth century. These impressive dams and vast lakes were created to supply water to Birmingham at the height of its population growth. While swimming is not officially allowed

△ 75

△ 73

in the reservoirs it is still possible to swim in the Elan at the pool where it meets the Wye a few miles downstream. In the spring the water flows in from the top layers of the reservoir and is not too icy. In summer the authorities begin to release water from the bottom sluices and it drops in temperature dramatically.

The Wye continues south from the Elan junction, often shallow but sometimes pooling where it meets rocky seams. Pen-doll Rocks at Builth Wells is a particularly impressive series of pools and rapids. Wildlife along this stretch includes ravens, red kite, buzzards, herons, kingfishers, peregrines and otters.

As it reaches the north escarpment of the Brecon Beacons the Wye is forced to turn abruptly north-east and arrives in the charming, bookshop-filled town of Hay-on-Wye, a place that loves to swim. The Warren, a twenty-minute walk upstream from the town centre, is the place to paddle, skim stones or watch hapless canoeists negotiate the rapids from the long pebble beach. Further upstream the river is deeper and a longer swim is possible. During the Hay Festival you'll find it packed with people from all over the world, propped up on one elbow reading with their picnics and Pimms.

These grassy banks had been used to catch rabbits since medieval times but in the 1970s a scheme was proposed to convert the Warren into a caravan park. Local businesses and residents were so horrified they decided to club together to purchase the field. A '20 Club', set up to find twenty supporters, quickly mushroomed into the '300 Club' that continues to run to this day. The outpouring of community spirit that was catalysed by this swimming hole led to other community initiatives and restoration projects. Anyone can join the Warren Club and membership is still £13, as it has been since 1973, though non members are free to use the area (www.wayonhigh.org.uk).

'Rocks piled on each other to tremendous heights, rivers formed into cataracts by their projections, and valleys clothed with woods, present an appearance of enchantment…'
Percy Shelley, on his walk to Rhayader, 1811

Upper Wye and Elan

73 Elan Wye junction pool

Town: Rhayader
Grid ref: SN 967656
Postcode: LD1 6NS (1.5km N)

Water quality: A
Depth/size: swim, dive, paddle

Walking: 1 min, easy
Train: Llandrindod Wells, 10km
Extras: Elan reservoirs

ⓘ A wide deep junction of the Elan and the Wye. Deepish section to jump into from bank. Shallower paddles upstream. Open and grassy. Elan is on reservoir release and can be very cold.

▶ 18km N of Builth Wells on A470 (or 5km S of Rhayader) turn L (R) over bridge and into Llanwrthwl. Go through village and up hill (600m), then turn R at T-junction. Follow narrow lane 1.8km to find bridleway on R, signed 'Wye Valley Walk', which leads to junction pool (50m) by bench and near footbridge. Follow lane on to reach Elan village and beginning of spectacular drive around famous flooded valleys.

74 Pen-doll Rocks

Town: Builth Wells
Grid ref: SO 032521
Postcode: LD2 3RD (100 S)

Water quality: A
Depth/size: paddle, swim, current

Walking: 2 mins, difficult
Train: Builth Road, 1km
Extras: Royal Welsh Show Ground

ⓘ An exciting stretch of the Wye narrowing through rocky cliffs. Downstream are safe white sandy bays. Upstream the water deepens through a small gorge with rock formations. Dangerous in high water.

▶ From central Builth Wells follow A470 N (dir Rhayader) over bridge to the roundabout in front of Royal Show Ground (junction A483/A470). Follow A470 exactly 1km, past garage and large lay-by to park in small second lay-by on L, opposite wide entrance to 'Penmaenau'. Find informal path L, over crash barrier and down steep wooded bank to river and Pen-doll Rocks.

75 The Warren

Town: Hay-on-Wye
Grid ref: SO 222426
Postcode: HR3 5YH

Water quality: A
Depth/size: paddle, swim

Walking: 10 mins, moderate
Train: Hereford, 20km
Extras: Bookshops of Hay-on-Wye

ⓘ A popular stretch of commoner's meadow by the side of the Wye. White shingle beach and shallows below the rapids/bend, and deeper section above. Tree shade. Good for paddlers. Beautiful setting. Rough track with parking.

▶ Approaching Hay-on-Wye from the west on B4530 turn L just after 30mph speed sign, into business park. Continue 200m through residential housing and, after road bends to R with speed bump, look for narrow rough track on L. Follow down for 400m to find parking. River is below, to L. From town follow the river upstream for 500m.

△ **77** Lady Falls in spate at Coed-y-Rhaiadr, South Wales

Waterfall Woods

Coed-y-Rhaiadr means 'waterfall woods' and you'll not find a more impressive network of forest lidos and falling water anywhere in Wales.

The route to the waterfalls near Pontneddfechan is found through an old gate inscribed simply 'Waterfalls' in wrought iron. Soon the sound of rushing water fills the woods. If you follow the trail for twenty minutes or so you'll come to a large rocky outcrop on the right above a mini canyon through which you can snorkel, with clear views of the underwater rock formations in the abyss below. Further on there's a large junction pool beneath a footbridge where families swim and older children jump.

Like many wooded waterfalls in Wales this valley has its share of legends. It was from a cave by the riverside here that Elidorus, a fourth-century priest, found a passageway to a secret land from which he tried to steal a golden ball. The next waterfall along, Sgwd Gwladys, or Lady Falls, is named after the daughter of King Brychan who ruled here in the tenth century. The falls occupy a giant amphitheatre rimmed with a lip of dark black gritstone. The great bowl holds a wide pool of gentle water and shingle beach. Moss and fern grow in profusion in this misty microclimate and many say this is the most beautiful waterfall in Wales.

I arrived at midday and the sun was high enough to light up the sunken woodbine and ragwort-draped glade. A slender chute of

△ 76

△ 76

△ 77

water was falling from a high ledge beneath slopes of oak and beech. Tiptoeing into the pebble shallows, I dove into the deeper parts of the plunge pool and swam underwater in the peaty darkness, hearing the drone of the water hum between my ears and the movement of the falls vibrate across my skin. Breaking the surface close to the far wall I clambered out onto a ledge of wet rock that leads around behind the falls.

Lady Falls is variable: sometimes it can be a roaring cascade, at other times a trickle. If you're well equipped and have time you may be able to bushwhack your way up a further kilometre through the forest above Lady Falls to find the falls of Einion Gam, named after Gwladys' lover. This is twice as tall, and its pool is cut into a sheer-sided ravine. Back at the footbridge and junction pool a rather precipitous path leads on to the Horseshoe Falls and two perfectly elliptical pools, like emerald lidos, lying deep in the forest.

In the parallel valley of the Melte, leading up to Ystradfellte, there are yet more waterfalls. At one of the most famous, Scwd yr Eira, an ancient drover's road passes behind the flow. In another the entire river disappears into the caverns of Porth yr Ogof, one of the largest cave systems in Europe.

This extraordinary landscape was laid down in layers of time. The oldest limestone was formed from the shells of sea creatures that inhabited the early tropical seas and these soft layers have been eroded into the plunge pools. The harder red sandstones and gritstones above were compressed out of the desert sands that covered the earth just before the dinosaurs and these form the hard lip at the top of the falls. Finally there are the carboniferous, or coal-bearing, seams, the remains of the first forests that colonised earth once the seas and deserts receded. Warped, compressed and contorted, all these eons of time are visible in the waterfalls.

78

Waterfall Woods

76 Little Canyon

Town: Pontneddfechan
Grid ref: SN 899087
Postcode: SA11 5UD (500m E)

Water quality: A
Depth/size: swim, dive

Walking: 15 mins, moderate
Train: Aberdare, 12km
Extras: Scwd yr Eira

ℹ️ An exciting and relatively safe piece of gorge swimming. A pool flows slowly through a deep, narrow channel, 5m wide for about 30m. There's a large rocky outcrop by path to watch from, or jump in from. Dangerous when flooding.

▶️ Pontneddfechan is 2km from Glyn Neath on the A465 from Swansea (or A470 Merthyr Tydfil from Cardiff). From the roadside Angel Inn turn L and find iron gates just before the old bridge into the woods. Follow the river on good path for 1.3km (20 mins). An open field and gate on L marks halfway. If you reach the picnic tables you've gone too far.

77 Sgwd Gwladys/Lady Falls

Town: Pontneddfechan
Grid ref: SN 896093
Postcode: SA11 5UR (500m S)

Water quality: A
Depth/size: paddle, swim

Walking: 25 mins, moderate
Train: Aberdare, 12km
Extras: Henrhyd Falls, Coelbren

ℹ️ A graceful column of water falls 10m into a deep, large plunge pool set in an amphitheatre in the woods. Swim beneath fall. Climb up behind fall and then dive back in.

▶️ Continue on from Little Canyon 500m and arrive at junction pool with footbridges. The pool here is deep and large and good for swimming. Cross first bridge and turn L (up Afron Pyrddin), past Lime Pool (300m) to reach tall waterfall with pool (450m). Flow can vary considerably and can dry up altogether, though pool remains. Access to viewing platform on L. Einion Gam Falls 1km upstream, no path (SN 890094).

78 Horseshoe Falls

Town: Pontneddfechan
Grid ref: SN 903097
Postcode: SA11 5UR (500m SE)

Water quality: A
Depth/size: swim, dive, current

Walking: 45 mins, difficult
Train: Aberdare, 12km
Extras: Ystradfellte and Porth yr Ogof cave

ℹ️ A fantastic set of deep forest plunge pools beneath a horseshoe-shaped waterfall.

▶️ Continue on from Little Canyon 500m and arrive at junction pool with footbridges. Cross first footbridge, turn R and bear L (up main river, Neddfechan) for a further 800m along an often muddy and steep path. The main pool drains into a second pool almost as big. In normal flows these pools are flat and relatively calm. Above the path leads on to Lower Ddwli (150m, SN 904098) and Upper Ddwli (400m, SN 906099) for yet more dips.

△ **81** Nant Sere waterfalls beneath the Brecon Beacons

Usk and Pen-y-Fan

The River Usk runs deep through the heart of the Brecon Beacon National Park, fed by the streams and pools of the Pen-y-Fan and Cribyn. Carving through soft pink sandstone, it is a shallow river for much of its length, but occasionally opens out into beautiful hidden swimming holes.

One such area is around the little village of Llangynidr, halfway between Brecon and Abergavenny, nestling on the edge of the high moors. From the narrow medieval bridge the river runs rocky and shallow below, forming small rivulets between island clumps of butterwort and shingle. The bedrock is as gentle to the touch as soapstone but struck through with cream and red quartz bands. Rounded eddy holes hold little piles of pebbles, and pillars of rock stand like miniature wind-carved tors, etched by the current and flow.

Picking my way down the rough bankside path from the bridge I was searching for a particularly idyllic swimming pool discovered by a friend. Just as I was about to give up and return to the bridge the alto tinkling of the shallow water began to lower into the baritone of a deeper pool. A few minutes ahead the river poured over a low ledge into an area of still water extending from bank to bank with flat sunny picnic ledges and sculpted stones on which countless local families must have hung their clothes.

This was perfect river swimming. I was surrounded by open fields yet shaded by a coppice of poplar trees hung with mistletoe. Scents of

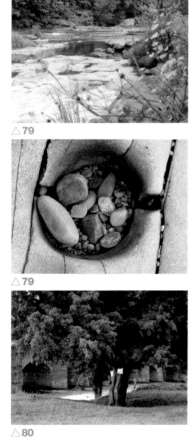

△ 79

△ 79

△ 80

wild saffron and mown hay hung on a late summer breeze with early evening birdsong, all inducing a sort of hypnosis as the water sung on by. I came round to the sound of a lamprey blowing bubbles on the surface. Dangling my legs in the water, feeling tentatively for the bottom, I dived in then struck out, swimming gently against the flow and letting a trickle of sweet water into my mouth.

The Vale of the Usk is a wonderful valley in which to while away a weekend of wildlife spotting. Bats may be seen in the late evening swooping over the river, purple- and green-winged orchids can be found and in the spring there are crab apple, wild cherry and plum blossoms.

Some miles downstream you'll find Crickhowell, a medieval town beneath Table Mountain – Crug Hywel – from which it takes its name. There is good paddling and plunging in the pool beneath the bridge and a small weir by some stone steps. An old right of way stretches across the river and if you swim across you'll notice that the bridge appears to have seventeen arches from one side but only sixteen from the other.

Upstream the great escarpment peaks of the Brecon Beacons are like turrets above the Usk valley. The ridge path along Pen-y-Fan is popular on a summer day but few know about the waterfall that cascades down into the Usk, set into the side of the steep mountain and invisible from above.

The valley of Nant Sere is the most remote: a series of moss-covered waterfalls in a deep, sheltered vale filled with patches of ancient oak woodland and shallow pools among mountain bracken. At least five falls drop down this mountainside and after a hard walk up to the summits there's nothing more idyllic than to descend and dip in every one.

Usk and Pen-y-Fan

79 Llangynidr, Usk

Town: Crickhowell
Grid ref: SO 152203
Postcode: NP8 1NQ (100m N)

Water quality: A
Depth/size: swim, dive

Walking: 15 mins, difficult
Train: Abergavenny, 20km
Extras: Llangorse sailing lake

ⓘ Two beautiful, secluded river pools in remote countryside, 30m long with smooth red, flat rocks, 2–3m deep with diving possibilities. Rough going on riverside path.

▶ Llangynidr is 9km west of Crickhowell on either B4558 or A40. Bridge is about a 1km NW of main village centre. From medieval bridge (not the bridge over the canal!) drop down and follow the river's R bank downstream 800m (about 15 mins) until you come to a low ledge waterfall which drops into large deep pool. Alternatively go upstream about 600m, also river's R bank, to find flat riverbank rock and deep pool (SO 148203).

80 Crickhowell, Usk

Town: Crickhowell
Grid ref: SO 215181
Postcode: NP8 1AR (100m SW)

Water quality: A
Depth/size: paddle, plunge

Walking: 2 mins, easy
Train: Abergavenny, 12km
Extras: Views from the Sugar Loaf Mt

ⓘ A large pool, up to 2m deep, beneath the arched medieval bridge of Crickhowell. Rather open and visible, but fun if others are swimming too. Also paddling and shallow pools for miles along path upriver from the bridge.

▶ Crickhowell is 11km from Abergavenny on the A40. Park in town and walk 200m down to the bridge. There are two steps down to the river from Bridge End Inn (river's L bank). Or follow path upstream for up to 2km to find more privacy. Good pub in town, Bear Hotel (www.bearhotel.co.uk).

81 Pen-y-Fan, Nant Sere

Town: Brecon
Grid ref: SO 026230
Postcode: LD3 8LL (2km SW)

Water quality: A
Depth/size: plunge

Walking: 30 mins, moderate
Train: Llanwrtyd Wells, 25km
Extras: Pen-y-Fan ridge walk

ⓘ A string of magical shallow waterfalls through fairy woodland under heather-covered hillside, under Pen-y-Fan. Some moss-covered. Pools up to 1m deep.

▶ Spectacular approach from Cribyn. Otherwise from A40 roundabout (W Brecon) head into town and after 800m turn R into Bailihelig Road by church. Follow lane 3.2km to T-junction. Turn R and continue 1km to road end. 200m walk up onto open moorland, bear R to follow contour alongside wall for 1.2km until it drops to stream. First waterfall is hidden under tree 200m straight ahead on contour. Follow stream 1km to find others.

△ **82** Pool beneath Wolf's Leap gorge, River Irfon

Wolf's Leap and the Cambrian Mountains

Wolf's Leap is a tight rocky canyon on the River Irfon set above a series of deep river pools. Rugged and beautiful, the valley winds its ways down from the rooftop wilds of central Wales and is a sanctuary for the once rare red kite.

The canyon takes its name from the last wolf in Wales, allegedly seen jumping to freedom here in the sixteenth century. Wolves were perceived as vermin and hunted to extinction. The same fate almost befell the red kite, which was down to just a handful of breeding pairs by the end of the nineteenth century. These mountains were their lonely refuge but a huge conservation effort has led to their UK-wide recovery.

The journey to these hills can feel rather epic. I made it in a conked-out 1979 campervan, driving in from Tregaron in the west, up and over twenty miles of narrow mountain lanes. My van overheated and was saved by a call to the AA from the lonely telephone box that stands at the junctions of two mountain roads high on the moors of Rhos pasture, a wetland mosaic of heather grass and bog.

The River Irfon appears as you descend down the Devil's Staircase, the landscape opening up into a wide crag-edged valley. The pools themselves are at the outflow of a small slot canyon, which forms the metre-wide Wolf's Leap. This narrow crack of churning water has cut deep down into the rock and eroded pot holes and chambers. The pool is small but deep with great sloping slabs of Cambrian rock, some of the oldest in the world.

Well known as a swimming river, the Irfon was once used by local churches as a place for baptisms. Downstream from the Leap is the wash pool, also used by drovers, for whom the river was the beginning of a cattle-herding routeway to East Anglia. Up to

△ **84**

△ **82** Lone phone box on Rhos moor

△ **82**

one thousand animals at a time would be brought by this pool, sometimes under the shepherding of just one man and his dogs.

Downstream, the tiny town of Llanwrtyd Wells was once famous for its natural springs. These days they have fallen into decline but in an effort to diversify and attract tourists, the town has introduced the world championship for 'bog snorkelling'. Competitors have to complete two lengths of a 60-metre trench cut through the peat bogs of Waen Rhydd in the quickest possible time, wearing snorkels and flippers, but without using any conventional swimming strokes. A triathlon has also been introduced, as well as mountain-bike bog snorkelling that involves cycling underwater through the trench. With over a hundred participants each year, entries have included snorkellers from Russia, Australia, New Zealand and Ireland.

At the southern end of the Cambrians is the Black Mountain, the most western end of the Brecon Beacon National Park. In this area of sinkholes and limestone karst, Llyn y Fan Fach is one of two high tarns that sit beneath the peak. For many centuries legend has told of a 'Lady of the Lake' who would rise shimmering on the first Sunday of August at two o'clock in the afternoon. Apparently she married a mortal, a nearby farmer, but returned to the lake along with his cattle after he hit her three times. In Victorian times the tale was so well known that whole families would climb up the mountain in the summer sun in the hope that she would appear.

I camped up here with a friend one midsummer. A wall of bare scree rises up on the south side of the lake and many miles of central Wales's most remote interior drops away in undulating vistas to the north. We ventured into the grey, glassy waters at the end of the day, just as the sun was becoming pink in the sky. Having reached the middle we watched in amazement as great sheets of summer mist began to roll in and surround us on the water. Our distant tents disappeared beneath the shrouded veil and great wisps of ghostly vapour rose slowly up the mountain wall. We made for the shore, feeling the lake might suddenly erupt in some supernatural horror and stood there shivering and waiting, peering out for our camp. And then, just as quickly as the mist had come, it was away, and the burning evening glow dried us as the sun sank like a fireball in the sky.

Wolf's Leap and the Cambrian Mountains

82 Wolf's Leap, Irfon

Town: Llanwrtyd Wells
Grid ref: SN 841548
Postcode: LD5 4TR (800 SE)

Water quality: A
Depth/size: plunge, dive

Walking: 5 mins, moderate
Train: Llanwrtyd Wells, 11km
Extras: Abergrwesyn Nature Reserve

ⓘ A series of deep pools, about 10m across and 3m deep, at the outflow a narrow, interesting slot gorge. Open, sunny, good for picnics. A valley of wild beauty.

▶ From A483 south (dir Llandovery) reach Llanwrtyd Wells then turn L after river bridge and follow road 7.5km to reach hamlet of Abergwesyn. Turn L and follow mountain road (dir Tregaron) 2.8km up Nant Irfon until rockfall roadsign. River below appears from narrow gorge into several pools. Gorge is 'Camddwr Bleiddiad', Wolf's Leap. If time, follow road to Llyn Brianne Lake (SN 804538).

83 Wash Pool, Irfon

Town: Llanwrtyd Wells
Grid ref: SN 859499
Postcode: LD5 4TN (200m SE)

Water quality: A
Depth/size: swim, paddle

Walking: 1 min, moderate
Train: Llanwrtyd Wells, 6km
Extras: Bog-snorkelling championships

ⓘ A wide, open pool at the end of a short gorge with shelving access, about 2m deep. Long swim possible upriver. Car park above grass for picnic.

▶ From Llanwrtyd Wells centre take Abergwesyn road, following river upstream, NE. Follow road for 4.6km. The pool is marked by a Forestry Commission sign (Wash Pool) and car park. Walk down to pool R to enter. Deep section continues upstream through gentle gorge. Wolf's Leap swim is further 6km upstream. Llanwrtyd Wells events include such delights as bog snorkelling, bog triathlon and bog mountain bikes on the Waen Rhydd bogs.

84 Llyn y Fan Fach

Town: Twynllanan
Grid ref: SN 804220
Postcode: SA19 9UN (2.2km S)

Water quality: A
Depth/size: swim, dive, paddle

Walking: 90 mins, difficult
Train: Llangadog, 15km
Extras: Carreg Cennen Castle

ⓘ A high lake in the shadow of the Black Mountain, legendary home of a lake nymph. Deep (18m) and cold (500m altitude) but not as cold as Llyn y Fan Fawr nearby. Fantastic views and sunsets (west facing).

▶ Twynllanan is 3km NE of the A4069 between Neath and Llandovery in the NW corner of the Brecon National Park. Arriving in Twynllanan turn R and bear immediately L dir Llanddeusant 2.5km via steep narrow lanes. Park here or continue up to Blaenau 2km. This road becomes a track up to the lake, following the Afon Sawddle (3km). Bring hill-walking gear.

△ **85** Upper pool of Rhaeadr Du, The Black Cataract

Fairy Glens, Gorges and Gold

During the eighteenth century the most northern part of Wales was still one of the wildest and least chartered regions of Europe. Yet it was increasingly renowned for its beautiful waterfalls and was in vogue among the adventurous artists of the aesthetic movement searching for the ultimate 'picturesque' scene.

One intrepid travel writer keen to cash in on this trend was the eccentric Reverend William Bingley, a peripatetic pastor and naturalist from Suffolk who had taken it upon himself to bring tales of the wild waterfalls of Wales to London. *A Tour in North Wales: Delineated from Excursions Through all the Interesting Parts of that Highly Beautiful and Romantic Country* was intended as a guide to future tourists. It was published in London in 1798 and sold over 300 copies.

One of his most memorable descriptions is of Rhaeadr Du – the Black Cataract – a 'horrid, dark chasm' in a little visited woodland near Maentwrog in the northern Rhinog mountains. The best time to go is in early September when the water has been warmed, the oak leaves are still green and blankets of moss cover the forest floor. Sheer, steep, rocky cliffs soar up, trees grow out sideways and buzzards circle above. Huge tangles of fallen trunks litter the river bed but a string of quiet pools lie between, as calm as glass.

△ 86

△ 87

The canyon is much more peaceful than when the vicar visited it 200 years ago. Upstream the gorge was dammed and the waters diverted in 1925 leaving the river almost empty. The result is eerie calm, but offers wonderful swimming and sunbathing on the large dried-up bedrocks.

Take the old coach road which stretches up the hillside past a slender and abandoned medieval coach bridge, overgrown with ivy. After a sweaty ten-minute climb, with the ravine on your left, you'll hear the gentle sound of falling water. Down through the trees a bobsleigh run of rapids tips a slender column of water over the chute of Rhaeadr Du and into a perfect plunge pool below. At midday the sun is high enough to light up the glade but the cold may be intense – you'll be lucky to do more than rocket around the pool a few times, squeal and scrabble out. With the surface of your skin dilating and blood reaching into the extremities of your body in a great rush this is cold dipping at its most therapeutic. Drying off in the tingling warmth, your skin stinging, the world seems sharp and clear with the muggy layers purged.

There are many other beautiful gorges and waterfalls in Snowdonia. The Fairy Glen near Betws-y-Coed has long been a place for the romantics, its picturesque qualities still much in evidence. A swim down its steep-sided gorge is a sublime and peaceful experience. And what could be more fairytale than swimming in rivers of gold? Deep in Coed-y-Brenin forest, accessible via the extensive network of mountain-bike trails, two waterfalls lie at the one-time heart of Welsh gold production. The gold from this valley near Dolgellau made Princess Diana's wedding ring and has been the royal choice since Roman times. The last commercial operation closed down in 1998 but there are still many old workings along the gorge. The most prominent are by the plunge pools of Rhaeadr Mawddach. The building here generated power for the mines and they say the old tailings still contain traces of gold. Why not try panning for some of your very own royal Welsh gold?

'In this cataract, which is surrounded with dark and impending scenery, the water is thrown with vast impetuosity… the banks closed in above my head, leaving but a narrow chasm, from which the light was excluded by the dark foliage on each side… I found myself entering, to appearances, into the mouth of a deep and horrid cavern…'

From Bingley's
A Tour in North Wales, 1798

Fairy Glens, Gorges and Gold

85 Rhaeadr Du

Town: Maentwrog
Grid ref: SH 667388
Postcode: LL41 4HY (2km E)

Water quality: A
Depth/size: plunge

Walking: 35 mins, difficult
Train: Llandecwyn
Extras: The Grapes Hotel, Maentwrog

ⓘ A beautiful wild gorge, off the tourist track, with 2km woodland walk to high waterfall with deep plunge pool. Other pools and paddles along the way. Shady.

▶ From A487 Maentwrog follow A496 (dir Harlech) 1.5km, cross bridge at tight bend and park by the hydroelectric power station. Follow Woodland Trust path for almost 2km (30 mins) until you reach waterfall viewpoint. Backtrack and bushwhack down steep forest slope to reach plunge pool at bottom. Although this gorge is below the decommissioned Trawsfyndd nuclear power station and lake, none of the water in the gorge actually comes from the lake.

86 Fairy Glen

Town: Betws-y-Coed
Grid ref: SH 801543
Postcode: LL24 0SL (200m SE)

Water quality: A
Depth/size: swim, current

Walking: 10 mins, moderate
Train: Betws-y-Coed, 3km
Extras: Conwy Falls

ⓘ A picturesque, narrow gorge with access for £1. Some large rocks to sit on and a deep section down the middle to swim through. The grassy junction pool is also good for a longer, sunnier swim.

▶ From Betws turn R onto A470 (dir Dolwyddelan, Blaenau Ffestiniog). After 1km, as road bends to R for bridge, turn L for Fairy Glen hotel and park. Follow path via river to grassy banks (200m) and large junction pool, 2m deep in middle. Continue on (300m) to bottom of gorge from where it is possible to follow rocks up into gorge, or swim upstream.

87 Rhaeadr Mawddach

Town: Dolgellau
Grid ref: SH 736274
Postcode: LL40 2LF (600m W)

Water quality: A
Depth/size: swim, current

Walking: 20 mins, moderate
Train: Barmouth, 18km
Extras: Coed-y-Brenin mountain biking

ⓘ A large deep plunge pool at this little-visited waterfall, set among the ruins of a former goldmine. Second fall of Pistyll Cain converges also with pool.

▶ From Dolgellau roundabout (junction A470 with A496, Barmouth) head N on A470 dir Porthmadog for 6km. At the straggling village of Ganllwyd turn R 200m after phonebox. Road drops and crosses bridge. Continue 1.8km to road end and barrier. Park and walk 1.2km on track, following dark river with small pools on right. Pistyll Cain down path on L or go over footbridge and climb down through mine ruins to much larger pool of Rhaeadr Mawddach.

△ **89** Blue Pool, Golwern Quarry

Snowdonia Blue Lagoons

The disused mine quarries of North Wales often fill with clear, blue water and appear like cobalt jewels on the mountainside. Two of the best known are the evocative Blue Lagoon near Llangollen and the Blue Pool close to Dolgellau.

These old quarry holes were cut into the seams of Silurian slate, which often occur intermixed with deposits of copper. The copper inhibits algae growth – normally responsible for the green colour of natural lakes – and gives the waters an ethereal azure hue that is further deepened under a blue summer sky.

I had heard rumour of the Blue Lagoon near Llangollen but had no exact directions and spent a thankless hour criss-crossing the mountain before the blue lake finally appeared in view, 100 metres below me, set deep in the core of a volcano-like crater. I scrambled down over scree with yellow hawkbit sprouting from ledges to reach the massive slate rocks that make up its shores. Swimming near to the cliff face with goggles on is an experience that induces vertigo. The old quarry wall plunges down to a lunar landscape of moraine and boulders that appears far beneath, wobbling in the blue abyss with almost perfect visibility. At one end there is a sunken red car, abandoned by joy riders, its scale and depth strangely mutated by the water. Many divers come here to practise their deep-water skills.

Although there was quarrying here as far back as the seventeenth century, operations only intensified two hundred years later with the coming of the canal and then the railway to Llangollen. Traces of

△ **88** The Blue Lagoon, Moel-y-Faen, Llangollen

△ 89

△ 89

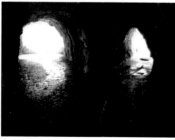

△ 89

buildings are still visible: dressing sheds, a steam winding house and sawing mill. Many years after closure the quarry holes have stabilised and the risks from falling rocks are no more than in any upland mountain terrain. However, the quarry walls are exceptionally steep and the water obviously very deep. Even though this is a popular place in summer you should take great care.

Golwern Quarry, the Blue Pool, is fifty miles to the west set high above the Mawddach estuary with views out over Cardigan Bay, Cadair Idris and the Rhinog mountains. You can walk up from Fairbourne or drive in via a spectacular mountain road from Arthog past the Cregennen lakes, although you will have to open at least ten gates! The pool is accessed via a short, low railroad tunnel which quickly opens out into an open-roofed cavern. This pool is smaller than Moel-y-Faen and almost perfectly rectangular with smooth straight rock walls that make it as close to a natural swimming pool as you can imagine.

The rich mineral seams of north Wales made many investors rich but just as many poor. The Prince of Wales quarry at the head of the remote and beautiful Cwm Pennant valley was a wildly optimistic undertaking. An entire village was built to house 200 workers, a tramway was routed for many miles up the mountain and a reservoir constructed to provide the constant water supply essential for running the machinery of a mine. You can still see the dam, a double-skinned dry stone wall that would have been filled with clay. The remains of an old waterwheel is some way below next to the ruined dressing sheds. Here the water-powered machines would have helped split and grade the slate before it was loaded onto the mountain railway. Although 200 years have passed since the reservoir was built it still remains, its pool of unused water perfectly clear blue. Sheltered in its little valley it is serene and romantic, surrounded by the fading ruins of a long gone industrial age with steep banks of heather growing along its edge.

Snowdonia Blue Lagoons

88 Blue Lagoon, Moel-y-Faen

Town: Llangollen
Grid ref: SJ 185477
Postcode: LL20 8DR (800m SW)

Water quality: A
Depth/size: dive, swim

Walking: 20 mins, moderate
Train: Ruabon, 15km
Extras: River Dee in Llangollen

ⓘ A very deep, completely clear azure blue lake at the bottom of a spectacular quarry crater (Moel-y-Faen). Steep scramble down. Steep cliffs all round. 100m x 20m lake.

❯ The Ponderosa Café and viewpoint is on the Horseshoe Pass in the Maesyrychen Mountains, 7km N of Llangollen on the A542 (dir Ruthin). From the café, cross the road and head up the hill on the main path. After 300m veer R into the quarry. There are two huge hidden pits with warning notices. The second pit contains the 'lagoon' deep at the bottom of its crater.

89 Blue Pool, Golwern Quarry

Town: Fairbourne
Grid ref: SH 621121
Postcode: LL38 2TQ (300m S)

Water quality: A
Depth/size: swim, dive

Walking: 20 mins, moderate
Train: Fairbourne, 1km
Extras: Cregennen Lakes and Cadair Idris

ⓘ A very deep, clear green–blue pool (50m x 30m) in a mysterious cavern entered via a short dark tunnel. Views of Cardigan Bay.

❯ 300m S of Fairbourne church (dir Tywyn), at telephone box, turn L up narrow lane. Continue 500m up hill. On R, just after entering the woods, find footpath to the R. This skirts quarry edge, entering it at the top. Find small grassy plateau and go through short (20m) straight tunnel to find hidden pool ahead. The adventurous can also approach from Arthog via the Cregennen lakes road and swim (SH 658144), which eventually passes above quarry (at least 10 gates on this route!)

90 Cwm Pennant

Town: Golan
Grid ref: SH 548496
Postcode: LL51 9AX (3.5km NE)

Water quality: A
Depth/size: swim, dive

Walking: 30 mins, difficult
Train: Porthmadog, 18km
Extras: Ynys y Pandy mill ruins

ⓘ A clear blue tarn in a hidden cleft, at the head of one of most remote and beautiful valleys in Snowdonia. Interesting old mine ruins and good hill-walking nearby. 20m x 100m lake.

❯ From Dolbenmaen, on the A487 from Bangor to Porthmadog, follow the signs to Cwm Pennant. Drive 7km to the road end of the valley and car park. Ruined house is above R. Follow path 300m up to it then continue up, bearing R on old railway, to reach ruined watermill and factory (SH 550433). Follow old stream valley to find old reservoir 200m above (www.penmorfa.com/Slate). Bring map!

△ **92** Lynnau Diffwys

Snowdonia Tarns

Tarns – or Llyns as they're known in Wales – are those magical lakes that appear as you're sweating your way to the top of the mountain. Swimming in them provides a total immersion in the landscape and the ultimate sense of the wild.

My favourite is Llyn Eiddew Bach, part of a series of wild mountain lakes that is very dear to me. It's in the heart of the northern Rhinogs, Snowdonia's least-visited region, close to a 300-year-old roadway that once linked Ireland with Stonehenge. I spent some time living in the farm close by and I would always leave a bottle of bubbly stashed and chilling on the lake bottom, tied to a secret piece of string, in preparation for weekend picnics. On the shallow side of the tarn are grassy, sheep-mown banks perfect for playing frisbee and paddling in the water. On the deep side are cliff ledges for sun lounging and for those who like to jump. A backdrop of bronzed September bracken, bony stone peaks and glimpses of the Irish Sea completes the sense of awe and beauty.

To the north, on the great massif of the Moelwyns and Cnicht, between Blaenau Ffestiniog and Snowdon, is another network of mountain-top lakes. Lynnau Diffwys are a pair that are rather shallow, though this does mean they warm up quickly. They stand at the head of Croesor's U-shaped valley, with views down the mountains, across the sandy flats of Traeth Mawr, and out to sea. You will also find nearby the crumbling remains of the mining town of Rhosydd, one of

△ **93**

△ **92**

△ **93**

the largest, highest slate mines in North Wales. There are over twenty tarns up here, all within a couple of miles of each other and you can make a fantastic ten-mile mountain walk from Penrhyndeudraeth through Croesor to Blaenau Ffestiniog, taking the mountain railway back to your starting point.

Snowdonia is a glaciated landscape and contains many true 'cwm' lakes ('corries' as they are known in Scotland). They have been scooped out of mountain walls by 10,000-year-old glaciers and are usually formed in a northern or easterly direction, in the shadow of the ancient afternoon sun. One of the most famous and dramatic is Llyn Cau in the deep cliff-faced cwm of the beautiful Cadai Idris near Dolgellau.

Getting in, and out, of a tarn like Llyn Cau is as much a part of the ritual as the swim itself. For me it has to be a dive. First I peer down to check for sea monsters among the rocky shapes of the dark bottom. Then, with a lurch of adrenalin, I leap in and am under the water, scrabbling up through a riot of rising bubbles towards the surface before breaststroking to the side, gulping little sips of the sweet spring water as I go. As I reach the shallows and wade out of the primordial depths my skin is already tingling. I may have only managed 50 yards but there's an unnatural sense of elation and achievement – my head is in focus, the world is in perspective again and all my grogginess has been washed away. No sooner am I dry then I turn to dive in again.

One branch of evolutionary theory suggests that humans spent millions of years evolving into uprightness as semi-aquatic waders and swimmers in the Indian Ocean – our subsequent life on dry land is a relatively recent and bereft affair. Here – in an expanse of wild water – I feel as happy as a salmon. The mountains tower higher, the sky stretches wider and the great unknowns of life wash over me. The rhythm and sensuality of the swim soothes the mind and carries stress away on its ripples.

Snowdonia Tarns

91 Llyn Eiddew Bach

Town: Harlech
Grid ref: SH 646344
Postcode: LL47 6YA (3km E)

Water quality: A
Depth/size: swim, dive, paddle

Walking: 45 mins, moderate
Train: Tywyn, 5km
Extras: Bryn Cader Faner stone circle

❶ A tarn in the remote northern Rhinogs, with cliffs for jumping and fabulous views of the sea. Good hotel for *après*-swim cream tea.

▶ From Harlech head N on upper road (B4573, dir Maetwrog). 4km, after bridge, turn R dir Maes-y-Neuadd Hotel (www.neuadd.com, 01766 780200). 800m, just before hotel, turn R up steep lane. Continue 1.2km to road end and parking. Follow track 1km, then across stile and a further 1km to reach lake on L (larger lake visible below on R). Bryn Cader Faner is a 3,000-year-old stone circle 1km north (SH 648353).

92 Lynnau Diffwys

Town: Tanygrisiau
Grid ref: SH 658466
Postcode: LL48 6SS (2.7km NE)

Water quality: A
Depth/size: swim

Walking: 90 mins, difficult
Train: Blaenau Ffestiniog, 5km
Extras: Rhosydd slate mines

❶ Two small shallow tarns at 500m at the head of Croesor valley. Fantastic views of Cnicht and the sea. Many other lakes and the ruins of the Rhosydd mine. Also approachable from Croesor.

▶ Tanygrisiau is 1.5km SW of Blaenau Ffestiniog. Pass under railway bridge and follow Cwmorthin Road (400m) then turn R onto steep, wide track. Continue 3km, pass Llyn Cwmorthin, bearing L until you reach plateau and old mine village of Rhosydd. Break off to the R (NW) over moor to find lakes (1km).

93 Llyn Cau, Cadair Idris

Town: Corris Uchaf
Grid ref: SH 718124
Postcode: LL36 9AJ (1.8km NW)

Water quality: A
Depth/size: swim

Walking: 60 mins, difficult
Train: Machynlleth, 13km
Extras: Dogach Falls, Tywyn

❶ A huge, dramatic glacial cwm in the crater of Cadair Idris set beneath 400m high mountain walls. It's a 350m ascent up from the car park, past numerous falls and pools, so even if the lake is cold you'll be warm when you arrive.

▶ 14.5km from Machynlleth turn L off the A487 onto the B4405 to find car park immediately on R. Cross bridge through woods and follow stream up hillside via major path to come to the cwm lake after 2.5km. The lake falls into shade in the afternoon. Complete the path up to the summit of Cadair for fantastic sea views.

△ **96** Llyn Du'r Arddu on Snowdon

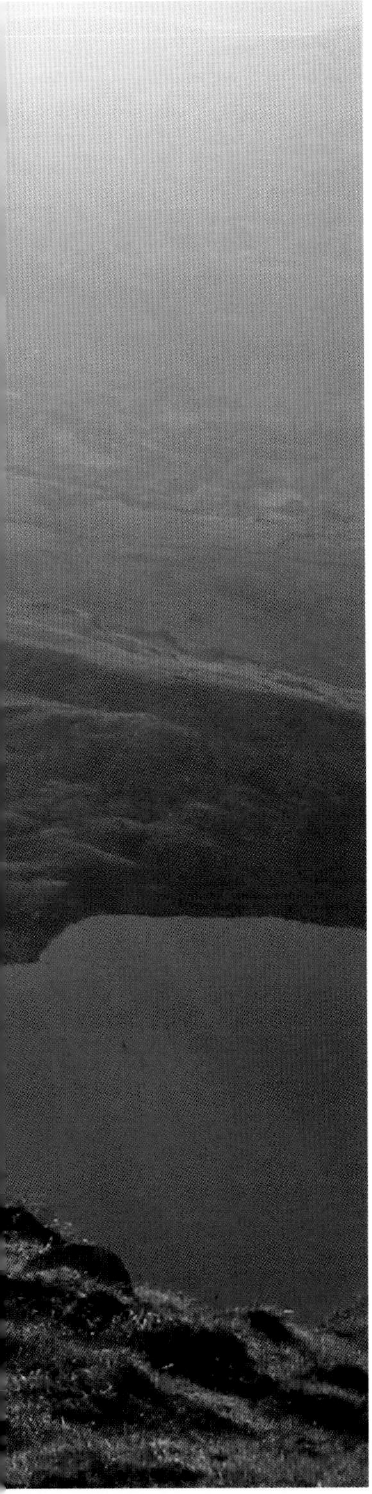

Swimming over Snowdon

Swimming over the iconic massif of Snowdon, with its pyramid pinnacle and stunning views, is the ultimate swim tour, with a range of dips from waterfall plunge pools to dramatic tarns.

The mountain has long been a place for wild bathing as well as mountaineering excellence. George Mallory, the ill-fated Everest explorer, was also a fanatical lake swimmer who used the mountain to train for the first British ascent. Accompanied by some of the finest thinkers of his time – E. M. Forster, George Keynes, the Huxley brothers, and other members of the Cambridge Apostles – an opportunity to bathe always rounded off a mountain day and complemented the new socialist ideology, which embraced a closer connection with the 'great outdoors'.

To swim over the highest mountain in England and Wales try this six-mile route from south to north, returning by bus and staying the night at the eccentric old mountain hotel of Pen-y-Gwryd. The route begins at Llyn Dinas under the precipitous rocky knoll of Dinas Emrys, a fifth-century castle stronghold where the original red dragon of Wales emerged from a pool and defeated the white dragon of the Britons. This crag-bounded lake makes an impressive and historic starting point and is lined with knarled oaks, craggy outcrops and parched gorse. Two miles up the road, at Nantgwynant, the Watkins Path begins. Within half an hour a series of large plunge pools and waterfalls appears on the right. Cascading down the mountain, deep blue and decked with rowan, this sunny, south-facing stream is popular with Snowdon walkers.

△ **95**

△ **95** Llanberis waterfalls

As you continue you'll pass more pools and the Gladstone Memorial where in 1892 the elderly statesman, after being prime minister four times, made a plea for justice for Ireland and Wales. The path turns and rises steeply up to the southern ridge of Snowdon and then on to the summit before heading over onto the Llanberis path that follows the course of the railway. From a mile below the summit you can drop down to the right, to the tiny tarn of Llyn Glas with its magical little wooded island. The tarn overlooks the Llanberis pass and the sea but it's a very rough, steep scramble (and 300-metre descent) to the plateau on which it's perched. Alternatively turn off left instead, to Llyn Du'r Arddu, a deep blue lake, stained by cooper and set under the craggy cliffs of 'Cloggie' (Clogwyn du'r Arddu). This 100-metre sheer rock wall is legendary among climbers and rescue helicopter pilots. So fearful is the location that legend says birds will not fly over the lake.

From here on down the River Arddu drains the heather moors for three miles and the path continues, tracking the railway, past Hebron mountain railway station. The road heads to the tree-line where you'll find another series of amazing plunge pools cascading into Llanberis. These are exactly one kilometre below Hebron station, just below the road, and 300 metres beneath where the railway crosses over the stream.

"Perfect weather. Explored Craig-yr-Ysfa, three new climbs, bathing each time on the way back."

Mallory's letters, 1907. He and his climbing partners took to bathing with obsessive zeal and wondered if life would ever be so good again.

You're almost home and after such an expedition you deserve a night at the classic mountain hotel of Pen-y-Gwryd, high on Pen-y-Pass. When Mallory and Irvine failed to return from Everest in 1923 it was 30 years before Hillary led the first ascent. Pen-y-Gwryd was where his team trained and it is filled with climbing antiquity. After a long day on the mountains enjoy the great Victorian bath-tubs, the outdoor sauna and swimming lake and a hearty five-course meal that appears on the dot at seven o'clock, announced by a gong.

Swimming over Snowdon

94 Llyn Dinas

Town: Beddgelert
Grid ref: SH 614495
Postcode: LL55 4NQ (2km SW)

Water quality: A
Depth/size: swim

Walking: 10 mins, moderate
Train: Penrhyndeudraeth, 16km
Extras: Sygun Copper Mine

ⓘ A 1km-long valley lake at the foot of Snowdon with stunning craggy backdrop. Accessible directly from the main road.

▶ From Beddgelert follow A498, dir Capel Curig, you will reach the Sygun Copper Mine (01766 890595) after 1.8km. Continue 500m to find road parking on L by Dinas Emrys. Cross road, join footpath to river, cross river at footbridge and continue upstream to reach non-road side of lake. To return at end of walk take Sherpa buses from Llanberis to Pen-y-Pass half hourly, and then from Pen-y-Pass to Beddgelert four times daily (www.gwynedd.gov.uk).

95 Watkins path waterfalls

Town: Beddgelert
Grid ref: SH 623516
Postcode: LL55 4NQ (600m NW)

Water quality: A
Depth/size: plunge

Walking: 30 mins, difficult
Train: Penrhyndeudraeth, 19km
Extras: Gwynant chapel café

ⓘ An extended series of pools and falls starting close to the Snowdon Watkins path. Rather overlooked but popular with walkers.

▶ From Beddgelert bridge, dir Capel Curig on A498, continue 4.8km along Llyn Dinas to reach converted chapel café (L) and car park beyond (R). Cross back over road to join Watkin's Path. Waterfalls begin after 1.6km.

▶ On the opposite side of the mountain the Llanberis waterfall pools can be found adjacent to the railway at SH 578593, just off the lane.

96 Llyn Du'r Arddu

Town: Llanberis
Grid ref: SH 601558
Postcode: LL55 4UL (2.5km SW)

Water quality: A
Depth/size: swim

Walking: 90 mins, difficult
Train: Bangor, 25km
Extras: Pen-y-Gwryd Hotel

ⓘ A deep blue lake set under a 100m steep rock wall, famous in climbing and traditional folklore. Beach on nearside, deeper waters at far rock wall. Arrive close to midday to catch the sun.

▶ From the Snowdon summit continue 1.5km down Llanberis path, following railway, until you see down below on your R the small islanded tarn of Llyn Glas (SH 619557). Drop down to this if you are feeling energetic or continue 500m to Clogwen station and turn L to Llyn Du'r Arddu. After bathing bushwhack along contour to pick up the Llanberis path again, 600m to N.

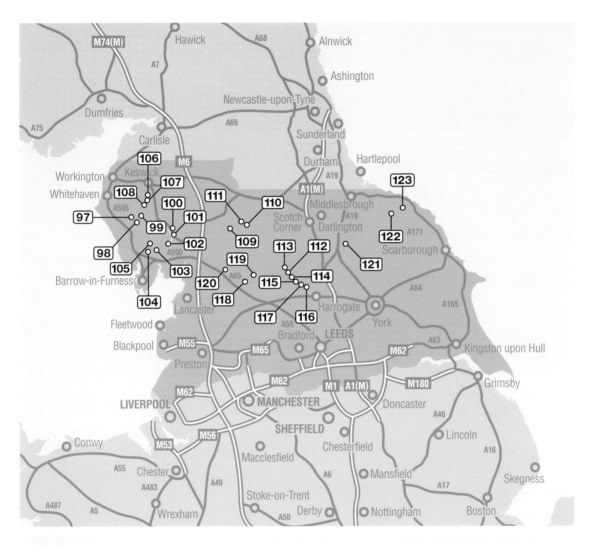

Highlights

97 Magnificent Wastwater: England's deepest, most dramatic and most beautiful lake. It also has an underwater 'gnome garden'

98–99 Eskdale: a magical series of pools leading up to Scafell Pike. There's nowhere better to be on a hot day in the Lakes

100–101 William Wordsworth's mountain pools with view across Rydal Water

103 Swim across to Wildcat Island of *Swallows and Amazons* fame

104 Ulpha Bridge: a fabulous family picnicking place from where you can watch the brave bridge jumpers

109 Hell Gill is thought to be a collapsed cave, now a semi-underground stream that feels like the inside of a whale. Descend if you dare!

110–111 Remote and wild: this is real Yorkshire Dales waterfall country – perfect for swimming

113 A gentle cataract great for 'tubing' – rafting the rapids on rubber rings

115 With two pubs, a river campsite and a tiny island, Appletreewick is an idyllic wild-swimming village

116 Set next to the ruins of Bolton Priory, this stretch of river becomes Costa-del-Bolton on hot summer days

121 The wooded Gormire Lake, set beneath the spectacular Sutton Bank, was a favourite location for James Herriot

Lakes and Dales

The Cumbrian Lake District, home to Wordsworth's daffodils and *Swallows and Amazons*, is a place of volcanic mountains and Lakeland islands. The nearby limestone karst country of the Yorkshire Dales provides a stunning assortment of waterfalls, gills and swimming rivers.

△ **97** Golden evening light falls on a small bay on Wastwater

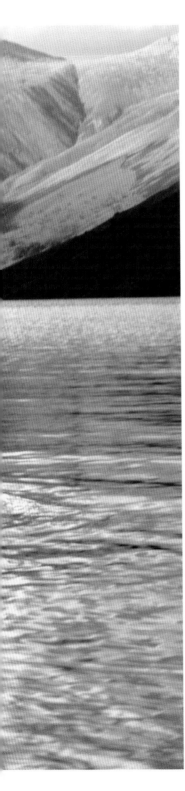

West Lakes: Wastwater and Eskdale

The sun was falling in golden pools in a small bay where a group of walkers and swimmers had congregated to catch the last rays of the day. Steep white scree slopes plunged 1,500 feet into the lake on the opposite shore.

Scrambling down to the shoreline, grimy from a day of driving, the cool water instantly quenched my skin. Striking out over the white quartz lake bed the water was as clear as the Mediterranean. Small clumps of freshwater grass were soon waving beneath me and the mountains of Whin Rigg and Illgill Head rippled in broken reflections around.

There are many little white bays along the three-mile length of Wastwater, several fringed with great boughs of Scots pine. The whole area is tinged with the pinks and blues of the white volcanic granite that underlies the area, a material so pure and hard that it creates virtually no sediment or nutrients, keeping the lake free of algae and the clearest in the Lake District.

This valley of Wasdale is certainly a place of extremes: Wastwater, England's deepest lake, is overlooked by Scafell Pike, its highest mountain. It even contains the country's smallest church so perhaps it's not surprising that it's also home to some of its tallest tales. The World's Biggest Liar competition was first won by Will Ritson, landlord of the Wasdale Head in 1872. The competition was resurrected by Copeland Borough Council in 1974 and has attracted competitors from Australia and Canada with classics such as the foxhound that could fly because its mother mated a golden eagle (1989 winner) and turnips so huge that the Lakes folk could quarry sheep pens from them (1992).

△ **99** Esk Falls above Tongue Pot

△ **99** Tongue Pot

△ 97

△ 97

△ 98

You'll understand, then, why I wasn't fooled by a story I heard that night about a garden of gnomes that lives 50 metres down at the bottom of the lake, guarded by a picket fence, which the police have tried to remove several times. As it turns out I needn't have been so sceptical. The lake is popular with divers and it's so clear and sheer that there isn't much for divers to do or see on the way down. A series of extraordinary artificial 'sites' have been built up to keep them amused and apparently the underwater gnome garden is growing.

The next morning I headed east to Boot in Eskdale on the other side of the great scree slopes, an area that shares the same bright white geology and crystal waters as Wasdale. Down near the road, a short walk from the pub, is a beautiful wooded pool called Gill Force. It's just upstream from a riverside church. The Esk is renowned for the magical pools and waterfalls along its 15-mile length and the higher you go the more dramatic they become. The next day I made a day trip high into the mountain to the legendary 'Tongue Pot' and Esk Falls, sampling many of the dips on my way.

Tongue Pot is just beneath the packhorse bridge at the head of the dale, about an hour's walk from the road. Here, in a cleft of the mountain burn, a long emerald pool has formed beneath a waterfall at the meeting of two rivers. A pebble beach shelves down on one side and an oak tree overhangs. On each side sheer rock walls rise up, making the place famous for jumps. The oak's knotty roots create excellent handholds for scrambling out of the water before diving back in.

Climbing higher, through Esk Falls, a series of perfect plunge pools extends right up to the Great Moss mountain plateau above which a shimmering Scafell Pike looms. Further smaller pots link back down again via Lingcove Beck, the rocks grey and sinuous, streaked with white quartz. Each forms a perfect place to lie in the sun as the waters roar by. When the sun is shining there is no better place on earth to be.

West Lakes: Wastwater and Eskdale

97 Overbeck Br, Wastwater

Town: Wasdale Head
Grid ref: NY 168069
Postcode: CA20 1EX (2km SW)

Water quality: A
Depth/size: swim, paddle, dive

Walking: 1 min, easy
Train: Seascale, 16km
Extras: Wasdale Head Inn

ⓘ Quartz-bedded, very clear, long lake (5km) with good shelving beaches and some of the most stunning scenery in the UK. Good pub and National Trust campsite.

▶ Wastwater is on the far west of the Lakes, off the A5995 coast road between Barrow and Cockermouth. It's also accessible from Ambleside and Eskdale via the hairy Hardknott Pass. There's access all along north bank via the lane but the best beaches are at 1.2km (NY 151053) and 3.8km (Overbeck Bridge, with car park on L by stream) measured from Wasdale Hall youth hostel (019467 26229).

98 Gill Force, Eskdale

Town: Boot
Grid ref: NY 179002
Postcode: CA19 1YG (1km S)

Water quality: A
Depth/size: dive, plunge, current

Walking: 10 mins, moderate
Train: Ravenglass, 15km
Extras: Boot Inn

ⓘ A small rocky gorge and pool on the Esk, close to the village of boot with its campsite and pub. Near the little riverside church. Shady. Deep section with rocks to jump from.

▶ Boot is at base of the Hardknott Pass or off the A595 south-west coast road and is a good place from which to explore Eskdale. From Boot Inn (www.bootinn. co.uk, 01946 723224) continue back down to the road junction (200m) and cross directly over down track leading to St Catherine's Church by the river (700m). Turn L, following river upstream for 250m to find narrow gorge and footbridge with pools below.

99 Tongue Pot, Eskdale

Town: Boot
Grid ref: NY 227035
Postcode: CA19 1TH (5km NE)

Water quality: A
Depth/size: paddle, swim, dive

Walking: 40 mins, difficult
Train: Ravenglass, 18km
Extras: Hardknott Castle

ⓘ A long series of fantastic pools. Tongue Pot is more dramatic with high jumps possible (5m deep) many small pools above. Kail Pot below is sunnier, shallower (1–2m) and more secluded.

▶ Park by telephone at bottom of Hardknott Pass and follow riverside path up through Brotherilkeld Farm.1km after farm (20mins), between Yew and Brook crags, and 100m after tributary on river's R, you will find the shallow but fun Kail Pot over wire fence (NY 218023). Continue on further 1.6km (30mins) to Tongue Pot itself, by path and 50m beneath old bridge. Further pools up Esk Falls (NY 226038) and Lingcove Beck (NY 228038).

△ **100** Beach of Buckstones Jum, overlooking Rydal Water

Central Lakes: Rydal and Loughrigg

The mountains, rivers and waterfalls of the Lake District were the literary inspiration for William Wordsworth and many of his influential circle. The area around Rydal Beck was the setting for many of his walks, swims and musings.

Rydal Mount was Wordsworth's base for eight years, his most beloved home, and the place from which he courted his future wife, Mary Hutchinson. There are many pools in the parkland and fells above Rydal but one was so special to him he named it after Mary and dreamed of building a cottage there.

We may never know the pool's true identity but he described it as 'far among the ancient trees' and I have wondered whether Buckstones Jum could be the place, set in open fells on the edge of the wooded estate. It's a perfect triangular pool with a shingle beach in a bay between two flat slabs of granite, the water pouring in over the rock lip and scouring out a deep pool, perfect for swimming. From up here a wide Lakeland vista opens up, stone walls criss-cross down the valley and Rydal Water glints below.

Wordsworth believed that nature was the crucible through which we must pass before our spirit can be independent. Many people who travelled to visit him in his remote home were touched by a sense of liberation and joy as they immersed themselves in the landscape. 'I have satisfied myself that there is such a thing as that which tourists call romantic... It was a day that will stand out like a mountain, I am sure, in my life', wrote Charles Lamb after spending

△ **102** Looking to the Langdale Pikes

△ **102**

*'Oh! many a time have I,
a five years' Child,*

*A little Mill-race sever'd
from his stream,*

*Made one long bathing
of a summer's day,*

*Bask'd in the sun,
and plunged, and bask'd again*

Alternate all a summer's day…'

From *The Prelude – Childhood*
by William Wordsworth, 1805

a day wading up waterfalls and streams. But returning to London he soon spiralled into depression. 'You cannot conceive the degradation I felt… from being accustomed to wander free as air… and bathe in rivers without being controlled by any one… I had been dreaming I was a very great man.'

There is an even more hidden pool above Rydal Mount, a grotto lost within the woods, and this might also be Mary's pool. As you climb from the edge of the park the faint path begins to twist through a dingle of small mountain ash and yellow iris. You can hear water rumbling and a rocky outcrop appears, dotted with yew, hawthorn and rowan. On coming close a carpet of moss leads down to a small stone bank, carefully constructed by previous pilgrims. The cleft is narrow and dark and the pool incredibly deep beneath the waterfall. Rock walls on either side provide places from which to plunge, and ivy and mistletoe hang down from the trees. Swimming in this deep bower, with the roots of the ancient yew dipping in the water, awakens a sense of wonder and intense elation.

Samuel Taylor Coleridge and Thomas de Quincy were also visitors to this area and Wordsworth would take them on rambles and boat journeys as they recited poems to each other. His sister records a July day in 1800: 'in the afternoon Coleridge came. Very hot. He brought the second volume of the Anthology. The men went to bathe, and we afterwards sailed down to Loughrigg'.

Loughrigg Tarn is still an idyllic setting, now with a campsite providing the most basic facilities. The tarn itself is a relatively small, warm and shallow lake, set in a grassy dell with rocky bluffs and woody copses under a backdrop of the Langdale Pikes. On one summer night I remember the sun setting in great streaks over the Tolkien skyline. Small groups had gathered. Some stood together whispering, others sat with guitars but one couple had slipped into the water and their bodies were sending perfect ripples across the still lake. Then they turned on their backs and just floated, gazing up at the sky as the clouds turned magenta.

Central Lakes: Rydal and Loughrigg

100 Buckstones Jum

Town: Rydal, Ambleside
Grid ref: NY 367078
Postcode: LA22 9LT (1.7km N)

Water quality: A
Depth/size: plunge, dive, paddle

Walking: 45 mins, moderate
Train: Windermere, 13km
Extras: Rydal Mount, Wordsworth's home

ⓘ A triangular plunge pool in the fells, open with large pebble beach and large rock slabs. Views down to Rydal Beck. Deep under waterfall (3m).

▶ Rydal Mount is on the A591 just outside of Ambleside. Park close to the house (www.rydalmount.co.uk) or inside if you are visiting (£6). From the church continue up the lane bearing L along the outside wall of the estate, past the last houses (300m) and continue on track alongside wall/woods for 1.6km (30mins). As track flattens onto base of fell you will see an obvious triangular pool on R.

101 Rydal Bower

Town: Rydal, Ambleside
Grid ref: NY 366077
Postcode: LA22 9LT (1.4km N)

Water quality: A
Depth/size: plunge, dive

Walking: 45 mins, difficult
Train: Windermere, 13km
Extras: Dove Cottage Museum, Grasmere

ⓘ A narrow dark cleft between rock walls and waterfall, crowned with rowan. Very deep (4m) and cold with cliff to jump from. Hidden deep in the woods with magical qualities.

▶ From Buckstones Jum continue downstream, through various waterfalls 400m to come to a large rocky outcrop, through which the stream flows. There is a small grassy entrance below and a tree to hang your clothes on. The pool is about 5m by 15m. It is also possible, but difficult, to approach following the stream up from Rydal Park, following the various waterfalls as you go (none good for swimming).

102 Loughrigg Tarn

Town: Skelwith Bridge
Grid ref: NY 346043
Postcode: LA22 9HF (300m N)

Water quality: A
Depth/size: swim, paddle

Walking: 10 mins, moderate
Train: Windermere, 12km
Extras: Tarn Foot campsite

ⓘ Beautiful small tarn, relatively warm, under skyline of Langdale Pikes. Basic but scenic campsite adjoining.

▶ 3km south of Ambleside on A593 (dir Coniston) find Skelwith Bridge. By hotel and telephone box, and just before bridge, turn sharp R up steep lane. 600m turn R and immediately L up farm track to Tarn Foot farm. Campsite (01539 432 596) is through yard onto field. If you are not staying at the campsite park on lane and follow footpath to right of farm, around edge of campsite on metalled road (400m), and across fence (L) onto footpath down to the tarn.

△ **104** Jumping from the popular Ulpha Bridge, River Duddon

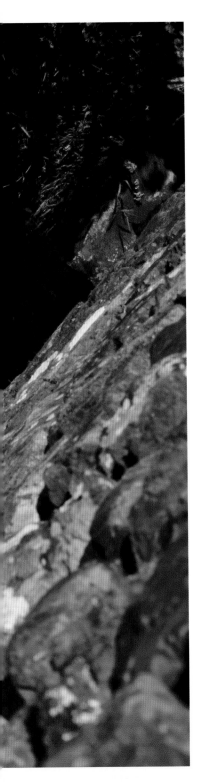

South Lakes: Coniston and Duddon

Peel Island – Wildcat Island in *Swallows and Amazons* – can be found off the south-east shore of Lake Coniston. Old woodland, gravel beaches and rocky promontories provide superb swimming, walking and canoeing.

Swallows and Amazons tells the stories of the Altounyan family who visited the Lakes over several summers during the 1930s. The adventures of Titty, Roger, Susan and John have captured the imagination of children and teenagers for generations since. Their adventures begin when they sight the distant Wildcat Island and mount an expedition to reach it. After learning to sail their clinker dinghy, the Swallow, they eventually reach the island and camp there, settling into a routine watching for enemies, making campfires and fetching milk and eggs from shore. Eventually they meet another group of children on the island who have a boat called Amazon, and they get up to various mischiefs together, drink ginger beer, go swimming, fight and bother Captain Flint on his houseboat.

Peel Island, is now owned by the National Trust and camping and fires are no longer allowed, though you will see many people sailing and canoeing there in summer. It is no more than 100-metres long and has steep rocky sides but in the south-west corner you'll find

△ **105**

△ **104**

△ **103** Swallows and Amazons

*'There are no natives on
the island now,' said Roger.*

*'They may have been killed
and eaten by other natives,'
said Titty.*

*'Anyhow, this is the best
place for a camp,' said John.
'Let's put the tents up at once.'*

Arthur Ransome,
Swallows and Amazons

both the 'Secret Harbour' and the beach described in the books. Anyone who has taken a boat in here, manoeuvred around the submerged rocks, splashed ashore and scrambled over the rocks needs little convincing that they are on Ransome's island.

It's from the beautiful rocky headlands in the woods at Low Peel Near that you can swim to the island, a crossing of some 100 metres. There are several other swimmable bays up the east coast but the most popular beach is on the western side along the grassy banks of Brown Howe, close to where the Amazon family had their home.

Arthur Ransome was inspired by his own childhood holidays spent in the Lake District. Each summer as he and his siblings arrived they would rush down to the lake, dip their hands in the water and make a wish. When they left they were 'half drowned in tears'. Nibthwaite, the tiny village where they stayed, is at the south end of Lake Coniston and still retains an air of simple, carefree summers.

Parallel to Lake Coniston, only eight miles to the west, is another valley rich with childhood memories. Ulpha Bridge on the River Duddon has also been a favourite for family swimming for generations. The grassy banks and cherry trees provide a choice of shallows or deeper pools. The little post office sells sandwiches, coffee, newspapers, ice creams and fishing nets. Many families while away whole days here and the bridge jumping – from a respectable fifteen foot – provides ongoing entertainment through the afternoons.

Further up the Duddon valley, craggy hills create a rugged backdrop as the road twists and turns, meeting the river here and there. Beyond the hamlet of Seathwaite are the rocky pools of Birk's Bridge on the edge of Dunnerdale Forest. Set in a canyon overshadowed with dappled sunlight and beneath an old packhorse bridge, the water is still, deep and clear. It's possible to swim right up and under the bridge into a small gorge underneath a waterfall. The road continues on and up to Hardknott Pass and the old Roman Fort, eventually connecting up with Eskdale and its string of swims, creating a perfect wild-swimming driving tour.

South Lakes: Coniston and Duddon

103 Peel Island, Lake Coniston

Town: Blawith
Grid ref: SD 295919
Postcode: LA21 8BL (700m SE)

Water quality: A
Depth/size: dive, swim

Walking: 15 mins, moderate
Train: Ulverston, 15km
Extras: Coniston Hall campsite

ⓘ A stretch of wooded rocky headlands with secluded sandy coves. Peel Island sits across a 100m strait.

▶ On the A5084 head N, dir Coniston, turning R after Blawith, then L to join minor road up E side of Coniston. 3km brings you to Low Peel Near and a beach beside road. Peel Island is just N and best approached from here through glorious bays and headlands of Peel woods. Park here or 1km further on at Rigg Wood car park. On opposite side of lake, A5084 3km N of Blawith, is Brown Howe with car park, PC, beaches and grassy banks (SD 291911).

104 Ulpha Bridge, Duddon

Town: Ulpha
Grid ref: SD 197929
Postcode: LA20 6DT

Water quality: A
Depth/size: dive, swim, paddle

Walking: 1 min, easy
Train: Foxfield, 10km
Extras: Broughton-in-Furness

ⓘ A popular area of grassy riverside with 300m stretch of pool and shallows, deep section under bridge from which the brave jump. Easy parking, post office and shop nearby. Pretty setting.

▶ From A595 heading W, pass through Broughton-in-Furness and take first R after A593, dir Ulpha. Steep climb for 5km brings you to parking (R) and Ulpha bridge. If crowded head downstream (300m) where there are more deep pools. Post office is 1km further on, on L, and sells a wide range of goods. If you get bored of rivers there is always the sea at Barrow-in-Furness and some nice coffee shops at Broughton.

105 Birks Bridge, Duddon

Town: Ulpha
Grid ref: SD 234993
Postcode: LA20 6EF (700m N)

Water quality: A
Depth/size: dive, swim

Walking: 5 mins, moderate
Train: Foxfield, 18km
Extras: Dunnerdale Forest

ⓘ A clear stream in a gorge beneath an old packhorse bridge. Swim upstream from the rocks to the waterfall. Beautiful but shady.

▶ From Ulpha bridge continue N, past post office and, after 300m, bear R onto small lane. Continue for 4.5km to Seathwaite hamlet and pub, then a further 4km to Birk's Bridge (a small cul-de-sac on L by narrow old bridge). Swims are below and downstream, easiest access from far bank. Continue 200m for more parking on L by modern bridge. Hardknott Pass is a further 3km and Hardknott Roman Fort (and Eskdale) a further 8km.

△ North Lake District dales and fells

North Lakes: Borrowdale and Langstrath

Borrowdale is considered by some to be the most beautiful valley in the Lakes. A steep-sided vale, running ten miles from its sources beneath Scafell down to the shores of Derwent Water, it is spectacular and remote, with waterfalls, deep pots and high tarns.

An old lady who lived on St Herbert Island in Derwent Water once told Beatrix Potter the story of a squirrel that swam out from the mainland to collect nuts each summer. The lake is scattered with wooded isles and the story and location became the inspiration for the *Tale of Squirrel Nutkin*, in which the squirrel and her friends built a raft of twigs and used their tails as sails to reach the island. Now the lake is a little too busy with ferries for my liking, though there are still plenty of places to bathe along the shore, and squirrels do still swim here.

My favourite swim is further upstream near Seathwaite. From this tiny village, centred around the very civilised Langstrath Country Inn, a steep track leads to camping fields along the banks of Langstrath Beck. Just 15 minutes further upstream is Galleny Force, a series of river pools, sparkling as they overflow, overshadowed by twisted and teal-green mountain oaks. They are not deep, no more than three feet in places, but make a great place to snorkel with their hypnotic array of underwater light and shade. Galactic bubbles stream over the waterfall and sunbeams laser across the sandy river floors. I spent much of my first afternoon in Borrowdale floating about in these crystal clear pools, burning my back in the sun as I chased minnows and gazed down on the great wobbling underworld.

△ 107

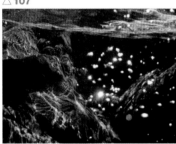

△ 106

△ 108

Beyond Galleny the valley walls steepen, peregrine falcons soar above the fell and the map marks the remote bluffs of Eagle Crag, Heron Crag, Bleak How and Great Hollow. Climbers report several caves in this vicinity and, a couple of miles ahead under the mountain eye of Scafell Pike, lies Blackmoss Pot, a cliff face above a wide cavity in the rock and a deep, clear cauldron of water.

The best way into Blackmoss is to swim upstream. The pot walls gain in height gradually so you have time to admire the curves and gain your bearings. This pot has long been a place of initiation, legend and superstition. In recent years teenagers have gathered here from Whitehaven and Cockermouth most weekends to swim in circles in the pool and dare their friends above to jump. It's not particularly high or dangerous – about fifteen feet – but many stand for hours trying to summon up the courage in vain. As any old hand will explain, you should make your decision to jump during a thorough reconnaissance beforehand. Then, as you approach for the real thing, you can clear your mind and step out, relaxed in the knowledge that there is nothing left to consider. If you dither at the edge, looking down and filling your head with dizzy vertigo, hours can pass in torture.

Beyond Blackmoss you can follow the river for several more miles as it becomes wilder and higher with more 'pots' and pools to find. If you follow it to its source you can complete the highest swim in England, on the edge of Scafell Pike at Lambsfoot Dub. Unfortunately it's only three feet deep so nearby Styhead Tarn and Sprinkling Tarn are more satisfying, far larger and just as spectacular. The temperatures can be chilly but no worse than a mountain stream, and the water tends to heat up through the day. Sprinkling Tarn has a small swimming island near the edge, linked to land by a causeway of stepping stones. From up here the views down Borrowdale to Derwent Water are sublime.

North Lakes: Borrowdale and Langstrath

106 Galleny Force

Town: Rosthwaite
Grid ref: NY 274130
Postcode: CA12 5XG (2km SE)

Water quality: A
Depth/size: plunge, current

Walking: 15 mins, moderate
Train: Penrith, 35km
Extras: Stonethwaite campsite

ⓘ Two sets of pools underneath cascades, about 200m apart. 1–2m deep, about 30m long. Fun for plunging and snorkelling. Rocks, grassy knolls and trees make it perfect for picnics.

▶ 1km after Rosthwaite (B5289) turn L to arrive at Langstrath Country Inn (1km). Very limited parking. If camping continue on rough track up hill for further 600m to Stonethwaite (017687 77234) and drop down to fields by river. Walk to end of campsite and continue on path above woods 800m to find first set of pools on L. Continue further 300m upstream to find river bend and pool below small fall.

107 Blackmoss Pot

Town: Rosthwaite
Grid ref: NY 267110
Postcode: CA12 5XG (3km SE)

Water quality: A
Depth/size: dive, plunge, swim

Walking: 45 mins, moderate
Train: Penrith 35km
Extras: Langstrath Country Inn

ⓘ A deep pot with 6m cliff for jumping. Interesting rock formations. Deep section for about 50m downstream. Upstream current under falls can be dangerous. Often teenagers at weekends. Fun, open and sunny. Many other pools further up Langstrath Beck.

▶ From Galleny continue on the river path for a further 2km until you see a rocky hollow by a fence, 300m after Blea Rock (the house-sized boulder on far L). Many more mainly shallow pools for another 1.5km upstream including Swan Dub and Tray Dub below footbridge (NY 264100). www.thelangstrath.com, 017687 77239.

108 Sprinkling Tarn

Town: Rosthwaite
Grid ref: NY 228092
Postcode: CA12 5XJ (2.8km S)

Water quality: A
Depth/size: swim, dive

Walking: 90 mins, difficult
Train: Penrith, 40km
Extras: Scafell Pike

ⓘ A high tarn in the shadow of Scafell Pike with island and excellent diving and swimming. Popular for wild overnight camping.

▶ From Rosthwaite follow B5289 3km and turn L to Seathwaite just before Seatoller. Park at road end and continue upstream 1.4km to Stockley footbridge. Cross and head up R side of Seathwaite Fell 1.5km to reach Styhead Tarn (420m altitude, NY 221099). Continue further 800m SE up to Sprinkling Tarn (550m altitude, NY 227091). Very shallow Lambsfoot Dub is at 660m just above Corridor route (NY 221084). Bring map and mountain walking gear.

North Dales: Hell Gill and Swaledale

I stepped down on to a remote and windy station halt. The train pulled away with a judder, creaking higher on the 'long drag' over the Settle-Carlisle moors. From here I would attempt to descend through the watery bowels of Hell Gill.

Hell Gill is a collapsed limestone cave system, now a deep slot canyon and geological curiosity. It provides the opportunity to plunge and paddle down an old underground river system, about 500 yards in length, without the need for specialist knowledge.

My local guide was Rob, an outdoor instructor. We climbed up Lunds Fell together, past Hell Gill waterfall and Hell Gill farm to a small medieval bridge spanning a deep fissure. This has long been a county border between Yorkshire and Cumbria: Dick Turpin leaped to freedom across it on Black Bess and Mary Queen of Scots was escorted this way to her imprisonment at Bolton Castle. Satan himself is said to have created this gash, which, though only a few yards wide, is like a fault line opened up by an earthquake. Ash trees overshadow crumbling sandstone cliffs, which almost touch in places. The water gushing in narrow chasms and pools below is heard rather than seen.

We entered further up where the stream tumbles down into the gorge via stepped pools. The sky was overcast but no rain was forecast and the whole stream catchment was within view, an important consideration when entering a slot canyon. The brown

△ **110** Lower pool

△ **111**

△ **109**

Slot canyons with long catchments are particularly dangerous as unseen localised rainfall upstream can create flash floods. Kolob in Zion Park in USA gained international notoriety in 1993 when a group of scouts lowered themselves into a flooding canyon with no means of retreat.

limestone karst walls were curvaceous and plump, undulating like an ileum, pitted with dimples making the water echo and our voices boom, as if we were inside Jonah's gut. The walls of the canyon rose higher as we descended, the light dimming, but the sky and trees remained reassuringly visible above.

I was only out of my depth at one point in a deep plunge pool that you must swim after sliding down a boulder by a waterfall. There is usually a rope tied to help you back up, should you wish to retreat, although if this is not there you should return and enter from the bottom of the gorge instead. There are also some accessible upper ledges to escape to in case of unexpected rains.

This brown limestone karst is found across the moors in Upper Swaledale too. The village of Keld has five excellent waterfalls with plunge pools. So remote is this region that in the seventeenth century the nearest consecrated land was over three days away. After following the river below you can walk the 'Corpse Road' back over the high limestone plateau.

Kisdon Force is the most spectacular set of falls with two huge pools beneath great basalt-like pillars, thundering deep down in the woods. The high pool is the larger, at least 100 metres across with ledges around its edge, while the lower pool is the deeper: dark and frightening with a steep walls.

At Park Lodge campsite in Keld, behind the café and down a track to a river, you will find several shallow falls flowing across hot, flat rocks with shallow pools that heat up nicely during the day. At night the campsite's riverside fires send reflections shimmering across the river pools and in the morning you can swim in your own private plunge bath.

Finally Wain Wath falls, a mile beyond Keld, is the most popular and accessible of the Keld swims. Prettily situated under limestone cliffs there's even a garden, a little gate and a bench on which to hang your towel.

North Dales: Hell Gill and Swaledale

109 Hell Gill

Town: Garsdale Head
Grid ref: SD 788970
Postcode: CA17 4JY (1.2km NE)

Water quality: A
Depth/size: plunge, paddle

Walking: 30 mins, difficult
Train: Garsdale Head, 5km
Extras: Buttertubs Caves

ⓘ A deep gorge with impressive rock sculptures, shallow stream, small waterfalls and midway plunge pool. Dangerous in high water. Scrambling skills required plus ideally rope, wetboots and wetsuit.

▶ From Garsdale Head follow B6259 (dir Kirkby Stephen) 4km and park by Hell Gill farm gate on R. Cross railway, turn L then R (100m). Note Hell Gill waterfall 100m below you on L (SD 778966). Continue up track 600m to farm, then 300m to bridge, 100m below which you will find Hell Gill exit. Or follow wood boundary 250m up hillside to find Hell Gill entrance. Never descend what you cannot reclimb.

110 Kisdon Force

Town: Keld
Grid ref: NY 898010
Postcode: DL11 6LJ (800m SE)

Water quality: A
Depth/size: swim, dive

Walking: 20 mins, moderate
Train: Kirkby Stephen, 16km
Extras: Park Lodge cafe and campsite

ⓘ Two spectacular waterfalls deep in a woody gorge. One is 5m high with 80m plunge pool, open and awe-inspiring. The other is 12m high with a 50m wide plunge pool, deep, dark and terrifying!

▶ From Keld village follow Corpse Road path dir Muker 800m then drop down to find Kisdon Force waterfalls in trees below. Also Park Lodge riverside campsite (01748 886274), falls and pools. If you are camping enter site through farmyard gate to L behind Keld teashop and descend to river. Catrake Force below (no access) but bathing pools 200m upstream in the ravine below Hogarth's Leap (NY 890014).

111 Wain Wath waterfall

Town: Keld
Grid ref: NY 884016
Postcode: DL11 6DZ (200m W)

Water quality: A
Depth/size: swim, dive, paddle

Walking: 1 min, easy
Train: Kirkby Stephen, 15km
Extras: Tan Hill Inn

ⓘ A wide waterfall, about 3m high, with pleasant plunge pool and open aspect. Limestone cliffs in valley and grassy banks for picnics. Interesting river and rock shapes downstream and good paddling.

▶ Continue beyond Keld (dir Kirkby Stephen) 1km. On R lane leads to Tan Hill Inn (www.tanhillinn.co.uk, 01833 628246) – the highest inn in Britain at 530m. Waterfalls are on R, 200m after junction and visible from road. Park on lane here. From Wain Wath continue further up the river to find other river pools and pleasant riverside campsite 1.5km further on, just before bridge on L.

△ **113** Tubing Ghaistrill's Strid, Grassington

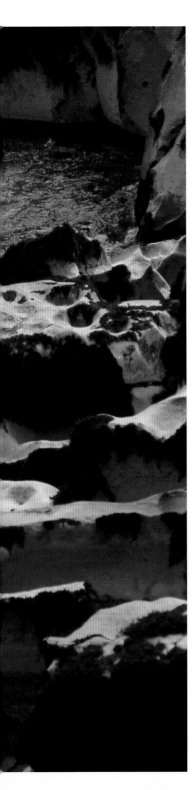

Upper Wharfedale: Loup, Grassington and Ghaistrill

Upper Wharfedale is the classic Yorkshire Dale: rectangular hay barns in every field, green meadows filled with wild flowers and beautiful rivers dotted with pools and falls.

High up on the fells of Moss Top and Chapel Moor the headwaters of the Wharfe begin to collect, filtering down through sinkholes, trickling through cracked limestone fissures before reappearing in tiny tributaries and streams. The Wharfe gathers pace through Langstrothdale then flows through the pools of Amerdale Dub before arriving at Grassington, one of Yorkshire's most picturesque swimming villages.

Most people gather on the river meadows to the south of the village. Here you'll find families in rubber dinghies and children wielding fishing nets. At the weir people slide down the smooth chute or swim in the larger clear pool above. Further down there is a waterfall by a footbridge and stepping stones to a riverbank church.

The connoisseurs, however, head upstream of Grassington to Ghaistrill's Strid, a series of cascades and rapids: the perfect place to while away the day swimming in rocky pools, chasing minnows and 'tubing' the rapids. Above the falls, and alongside an idyllic grassy knoll, the river is forced down a 100-metre bobsleigh run. Only a modicum of skill is needed to navigate the chute – the current takes care of the rest. The best method is to lie down head first on the ring so you can steer yourself with your arms – if you sit on the ring you

△ 112

△ 112

△ 114

tend to spin round and round. Our group was soon running time trials for sets of three descents, including the run back up the hill.

If you're very daring, and the river is low, it's possible to surf the white water without a ring at all, though you may end up bruising a knee or an elbow. Keep your head down, eyes up and arms in front. Stay streamlined but flexible and let the current curl you around the corners and guide you around any obstacles. The trick is to move with the flow like an eel and make only small body adjustments.

The walk from Grassington downstream follows an avenue of sycamores and oaks before arriving in the outskirts of Burnsall at Loup Scar, a faintly Jurassic-like limestone scar. You might well be disturbed by the spectacle of young men throwing themselves off the cliffs of the scar into the plunge pool below as part of a well known local rite of passage. The small pool is certainly deep enough for those who wish to test their mettle, but the full jump requires a degree of judgement as an overhanging cliff must be cleared. There have no doubt been serious accidents here. If there are no jumpers the pool is also excellent for a gentle swim and you can sit with your legs dangling in the water over its perfect edge almost as if you are at a properly excavated swimming pool.

Just below the rapids there is a larger river pool before passing behind the old Anglo-Saxon church of St. Wilfred's and heading on to the village bridge. On hot days the village green in Burnsall heaves with families. The field next door is turned into a large car park and the river is choked with a flotilla of the kiddy dinghies sold from the village shop and various makeshift stalls. The shallows below the bridge are popular with children, while upstream, alongside the pub, you can even find grown men drifting around in toy boats while ordering drinks from the bar.

Upper Wharfedale: Loup, Grassington and Ghaistrill

112 Grassington Weir

Town: Grassington
Grid ref: SE 000634
Postcode: BD23 6BG

Water quality: A
Depth/size: swim, chute

Walking: 10 mins, easy
Train: Skipton, 16km
Extras: St Michael and All Angels church

ⓘ A large grassy area of riverside common with two weirs and a waterfall plus footbridge. Popular, sociable and safe. Good swimming above higher weir and smooth chute (slide) on far side by ruined millhouse.

▶ Grassington is on B6265 13km N of Skipton. Park in Grassington village centre and walk down to the river via Sedber Lane (200m), or park S of the village on Church Lane which is next to Linton Falls and footbridge. Church Lane also leads onto the stepping stones by the twelfth-century church of St Michael and All Angels, set on the riverbank (SE 005632).

113 Ghaistrill's Strid

Town: Grassington
Grid ref: SD 991645
Postcode: BD23 5BS (200m N)

Water quality: A
Depth/size: swim, current, chute

Walking: 20 mins, moderate
Train: Skipton, 16km
Extras: Lower Grass Woods

ⓘ Exciting rocky pools and rapids. Lower pools have interesting snorkelling and a large reach for a longer swim. Also little tubs of warmer standing water in rockpools. Upstream rapids have a chute which is fun on rings but be careful!

▶ From the river bridge just outside Grassington, follow river upstream on river's L bank for 1km to come to the Strid: flat rocky ledges and pools beneath rapids. Watch out for submerged ledges. Upper section accessed by riverside footpath behind hedges, 200m upstream, to find chute, picnic spot and pool. Continue another 300m to Lower Grass Woods.

114 Loup Scar

Town: Burnsall
Grid ref: SE 031618
Postcode: BD23 6BN (200m NW)

Water quality: A
Depth/size: swim, dive, paddle

Walking: 10 mins, easy
Train: Skipton, 11km
Extras: Campsite opposite church

ⓘ A fantastic stretch of grassy riverside incorporating the limestone cliffs and plunge pool of Loup Scar and the shallower, larger, grassy river pool just downstream.

▶ Burnsall is 4km SE of Grassington on B6160 and 10km N of the A59. If you cannot park near the church you may need to pay to park in field by the bridge. A path runs down the L side of the church to the river. Turn L up the river (150m), up some steps and a further 200m leads to grassy banks and pool. Loup Scar gorge is 50m beyond with small, very deep plunge pool.

△ **117** Quiet pools beneath the notorious 'Strid'

Lower Wharfedale: Bolton, Strid and Appletreewick

Appletreewick is a delightful stretch of Lower Wharfedale with two pubs, some houses and a pleasant lane that leads down through grassy fields to a river pool with an island.

Bathing morning and dusk in this peaceful place became the routine of our days. I had arranged to explore the area and test out the local swimming holes with a group of friends. Emerging from our tents we would slowly gather at breakfast time beneath the old hazel, dive into the cool peaty waters and swim several lengths of the long pool. Then we would loll about on the short grass and dry in the morning sun, sipping tea and reading papers, sometimes putting up a hammock between the trees if we felt energetic. Soon we were planning the day's excursion but by dusk we would re-congregate, sometimes lighting up the island with candle lanterns and swimming silently in the inky waters beneath the rising stars.

Downstream of our happy home at Appletreewick is the Bolton Abbey estate and we made several expeditions to test the waters and teashops there. The great ruins of this major monastic enclave sit on a bend of the river above a stretch of pebbly beaches. During the hottest days it becomes a Yorkshire Costa del Sol: a mass of swimmers and sunbathers mixed with suntan lotion and sloppy ice cream. Upstream the river is deep enough for swimming,

△ **115** Appletreewick by night

△ **116**

△ **115**

downstream it is shallow enough for paddling and stone skimming. Taking the water, ruins and landscape together it's not surprising it attracts so many people.

Some miles upstream the 'Strid' section of river is less crowded. The river here runs through a notorious cataract with fantastical curving rock shapes. The water is so deep that it is almost motionless on the surface. When in flood the level rises quickly creating treacherous under-surface eddies. Although the Strid is very narrow it is 20 feet deep in places and its profile is hourglass shaped. Underwater there are many hidden caves and pockets in which you would not want to get trapped.

A 'strid' in old provincial English literally means 'a narrow passage between precipitous rocks or banks, which looks as if it might be crossed at a stride'. A number of people have died trying to jump the gap, or venturing too close to the edge, and the dangers are particularly acute during heavy rains.

We peered into the Strid respectfully and decided to swim several hundred yards below it instead, where the river has returned to its normal width. The bluebell-rich beach and oak woods have been opened up by a series of tracks and are a Site of Special Scientific Interest, renowned for their African summer migrants including the wood warbler, redstart and pied flycatcher. Arriving by the middle of May they find the insect-rich vegetation and mild valley climate irresistible. The yellow and white wood warbler nests at ground level and can be hard to spot, though its call of a whistle followed by a harsh trill is difficult to miss. The pied flycatcher is scarce, though nesting boxes have been placed around the woods.

We swam breaststroke under the lush beech trees while a warbler whistled sweetly from the bank. Some of us swam up close to the Strid and peered in from the safety of our downstream position. The curving rocks rose up above us and we thought soberly of the water's potential power and fury.

Lower Wharfedale: Bolton, Strid and Appletreewick

115 Appletreewick

Town: Appletreewick
Grid ref: SE 053597
Postcode: BD23 6DD (200m S)

Water quality: A
Depth/size: swim, dive, chute

Walking: 10 mins, easy
Train: Skipton, 12km
Extras: Mason's Farm campsite

ℹ️ A pretty rocky pool in the river with a small island and bay and rapids upstream. Rope swing on far side, grassy banks and field for picnics. Large shingle beach on far bank downstream too. The water has many submerged underwater rocks, which makes diving dangerous and swimming sometimes difficult.

▶️ Appletreewick is 3km off the B6160 via Bolton Abbey and the A59 from Skipton. Opposite the New Inn follow the track down the field to the river; pool is 200m downstream. Camp by the river (01756 720275) or stay at the more upmarket Craven Arms (01756 720300), just up the road from the New Inn.

116 Bolton Abbey

Town: Bolton Abbey
Grid ref: SE 075542
Postcode: BD23 6AL (100m E)

Water quality: A
Depth/size: swim, paddle

Walking: 5 mins, easy
Train: Skipton, 7km
Extras: Priory ruins

ℹ️ A popular stretch of river in front of the priory ruins. Upstream of stepping stones and bridge is deeper section where people sometimes use boats. Downstream are the shallows but underground rocks make swimming difficult and diving dangerous.

▶️ From Skipton follow A59 (dir Harrogate) 10km. Turn L at roundabout B6160 (dir Grassington) and Bolton Abbey village is after 2km. Park car on L, cross road and descend into estate through gates. River is in front of ruin (www.boltonabbey.com). Tearoom and restaurant 1km upstream at The Pavillion. The Strid is upstream.

117 Strid Woods

Town: Bolton Abbey
Grid ref: SE 067562
Postcode: BD23 6AN (400m NW)

Water quality: A
Depth/size: swim

Walking: 15 mins, moderate
Train: Skipton, 12km
Extras: Strid Woods nature reserve

ℹ️ A shady, deep stretch of river beneath the notorious Strid gorge (do not swim IN the cataract itself). Wide river shelving gently to 3m. Stony bottom. Dappled and glorious on a sunny day. A long swim possible up to entrance of Strid and downstream until it shallows. At weekends the path alongside river can be busy.

▶️ 3km beyond Bolton Abbey, find turning R into The Strid caravan park and car park. Pay for parking and walk down through woods to admire the cataract. Follow path downstream to about 300m beneath end of the cataract and drop down to rocky riverside.

△ **119** Cowside Beck north of Malham Tarn

Ribblesdale, Ingleton and Malham

The Yorkshire Dales have more waterfall plunge pools than anywhere else in England. The south-west corner of the Dales, around Settle and Ribblesdale, is one of best-known areas.

At Stainforth on the River Ribble, just a few miles north of Settle, a caravan park has grown up around one of the river's most popular swimming holes. It's always busy through the summer and deservedly so. There is a series of shallow rapids by an old packhorse bridge where children fish and paddle. The water then tumbles down a waterfall into a deep, black, smooth-sided plunge pot with an old iron ladder. On any day in summer you can sit and watch the antics of children and parents alike testing their nerve by jumping into the cauldron from higher and higher vantage points. Downriver, fields open out in a wash of peace and buttercups, and further large pools provide a place for longer swims.

Catrigg Force is just a mile's walk from Stainforth but much more secret. Water squeezes down through a slot in the tall rock structure via an upper pool, into which you can climb, and down into the lower pool. It's only large enough for a quick plunge but the cathedral-like setting deep in this wooded glade more than makes up for that in awe and wonder.

△ **118**

△ **119** Catrigg

△ **120** Beezley Falls, Ingleton

The reason for all these waterfalls is the limestone geology and the legacy of glaciation. At Gordale Scar, ten miles away, a 400-foot-deep ravine is all that remains of a great underground river cave the size of the Channel Tunnel, while nearby at Malham Cove a waterfall with the power of Niagara once flowed over a vast inland cliff. This cliff can still be seen, stained grey and overgrown with ferns and shrubs. Several miles upstream Malham Tarn, a mile-wide lake, is all that remains of the great river that once fed it. It is now a wildlife reserve with possibilities for discreet swimming among the curlews, mallards and greater crested grebe that live there.

For more waterfalls than you can possibly swim in a day you should try the Ingleton waterfall walk, on a par with the Coed-y-Rhaiadr walks in South Wales. Thousands of visitors travelled by the new railway from Manchester and Bradford on its opening in April 1885 to see the geological wonders. By 1888 it was attracting over 3,000 visitors a day, even with an entrance price of 2d.

On the western side Pecca Falls and Thornton Force are now in open-access land though no one will thank you for attempting to park in these narrow lanes. Thornton Force is more popular, a classic strata waterfall with an upper layer of 330 million-year-old carboniferous Great Scar limestone and lower layers of 500 million-year-old Ordovician sandstone. The pool is open, south-facing and on a hot day you will find many people wading, swimming and clambering on the rocks. Pecca Falls below flows through a woody glen and its many plunge pools will be attractive if you're a Gollum-type that likes to scrabble on the rocks and dive in and fish among the dark pools.

Ribblesdale, Ingleton and Malham

118 Stainforth Force

Town: Stainforth
Grid ref: SD 818671
Postcode: BD24 9QD (200m SW)

Water quality: A
Depth/size: swim, dive, paddle

Walking: 15 mins, easy
Train: Settle, 5km
Extras: Craven Heifer Hotel

ⓘ A series of river pools and falls set beneath an old packhorse bridge. Grassy banks and good paddling. A deep cauldron into which the brave jump. Longer river pools. Set below a caravan park though peaceful stretches in the field downstream. Peaty water.

◗ Stainforth is 5km N of Settle on R side of the B6479. Park in village and carry on up main road 200m on foot. Turn L down lane (Dog Hill Brow) and descend 400m to bridge (where there is also some limited parking in the off-season). Main fall is 200m downstream. Continue below this for 400m to find further deep river pools and more open countryside.

119 Catrigg and Malham

Town: Stainforth
Grid ref: SD 832671
Postcode: BD24 9QD (1km SE)

Water quality: A
Depth/size: plunge

Walking: 30 mins, moderate
Train: Skipton, 12km
Extras: Malham Cove, Gordale Scar

ⓘ An atmospheric waterfall set in woodland on edge of moor with small pool beneath towering rocks.

◗ From post office in Stainforth continue to green (100m) and turn R up lane, becoming a track up hillside. After 1km falls are below on L at top of woodland. Malham Tarn (SD 895663): from Stainforth church, find Goat Lane out of village up steep hill. Turn R after 1.8km then continue 6.8km to find parking 300m after Low Trenhouse Farm. Tarn is 300m up footpath on L, access from east bank only (www.malhamdale.org.uk).

120 Ingleton Waterfalls

Town: Ingleton
Grid ref: SD 695753
Postcode: LA6 3JH (600m W)

Water quality: A
Depth/size: plunge

Walking: 45 mins, moderate
Train: High Bentham, 6km
Extras: Ingleton Waterfall Walk

ⓘ A busy walk with concrete gangways but many spectacular pools if you don't mind the crowds. Thornton Force is most popular for swimming/wading.

◗ Ingleton is off A65 between the M6 and Skipton. Park and pay (£4) at Waterfalls Walk car park entrance, well signed (www.ingletonwaterfallswalk.co.uk). Follow clear riverside path to Pecca Falls (2km, SD 695749), a long series of woody pools, and then (a further 600m) Thornton Force, an open pool beneath a large fall. Continue on whole walk (further amazing swim in large cauldron pot beneath Beezley Falls, SD 705747) or exit via open-access land to E and W.

Yorkshire Moors

Sutton Bank offered the finest view in England according to the real James Herriot. From here you can see for miles across the Vale of York to the Dales. Halfway down the escarpment, romantically nestled in the woods, is the emerald oval of Gormire Lake.

The water of Gormire Lake is pretty warm and you'll most likely be the only person swimming there when you go This is a quiet and secluded place to visit among broad-leaved woodlands: a breeding place for coot, great grebe and mallard, sheltered by higher ground. A steep path leads down Sutton Bank, the top of the escarpment. Alf Wight, better known by his fictional name James Herriot, and his partner Siegfried Farnon had their veterinary practice in Thirsk (Darrowby in the books) about five miles away. He often visited Gormire Lake.

The tarn was formed 20,000 years ago by glacial erosion, and folk tales and legends of Gormire abound, many involving horses. One tells of a local knight who tricked the Abbot of Rievaulx into lending him his white mare. The mare would not respond to his commands, jumped off Sutton Bank and plunged him into the lake with the Abbot behind transformed into the devil. Ambitious schoolmaster John Hodgson was so inspired by this tale and a recent trip to the white horses of Wiltshire that in 1857 he and 31 volunteers decided

△ 121

△ 122

△ 123

to carve out their own horse from the escarpment. It was badly damaged by a hail storm in 1896 and fell into disrepair after the First World War but was renewed in 1925 and today is the most northerly white horse in England.

The steep, twisting road that leads up to Sutton Bank threatens horrible things to caravans as it rises onto the Yorkshire Moors proper. From here 40 miles of heather and gorse flow in undulating ridges to the sea. There are few large rivers but several smaller becks and woodland waterfalls near the coast at Whitby. One of the best falls is just below the famous village of Goathland, through which the North Yorkshire Moors Railway steams. Goathland is the setting for TV's *Heartbeat* and the station was also used for Hogsmead's Station in the Harry Potter films – the shop on the platform was transformed into the Prefects' Room and the Ladies toilets became the Wizards' Room. The Thomason Foss waterfall is approached from the picturesque Becks Hole pub and bridge a mile down the road. It's a short walk up through woods to a west-facing rocky pool in a sunlit glade, where families often come to play in rubber dinghies and swim under the falls.

Even closer to Whitby, on the other side of the A169, is Falling Foss, romantically set in deep woods by the fairy-tale cottage of Midge Hall. Set over a deep black chasm into which a small stream flows, smoke was billowing from the chimney and in the evening light it was a scene reminiscent of *Hansel and Gretel*. It's a fair trek to reach the bottom of the falls, backtracking and then picking a way along the overgrown stream bed. Standing on the shingle beach looking up, the waterfall flows down the jet black cliff like a white veil, breaking into hundreds of competing rivulets.

We dived in and swam over to sit on the ledges beneath the water. In the cooling evening air this was certainly a cold dip but the dark green mosses and jungle-like setting made this place feel strangely exciting: like finding a secret passageway to a lost world.

Yorkshire Moors

121 Gormire Lake

Town: Thirsk
Grid ref: SE 504833
Postcode: YO7 2EH (1.2km W)

Water quality: B
Depth/size: swim

Walking: 30 mins, moderate
Train: Thirsk, 12km
Extras: Sutton Bank walk

ℹ️ A large (300m), warm and little-visited lake set in woodland beneath the Sutton Bank escarpment. Squidgy leaf litter mulch at first but water shelves quickly, deepening about 5m offshore. Beautiful views back up to escarpment.

▶️ 10km from Thirsk (A170, dir Scarborough), after the long climb (no caravans) park and pay at main Sutton Bank car park (café here too). Walk along bank and after 300m follow signs to nature reserve to descend on track L into woods. Descend 500m to find lake shore among trees. There are public footpaths around whole lake and a permanent right of way on the south side.

122 Thomason Foss

Town: Goathland
Grid ref: NZ 826022
Postcode: YO22 5LE (500m E)

Water quality: A
Depth/size: plunge

Walking: 15 mins, moderate
Train: Grosmont, 4km
Extras: North Yorkshire Moors Railway

ℹ️ A plunge pool (20m) set beneath an impressive waterfall at the head of a woodland walk. Starting point at Beck Hole is picturesque.

▶️ Goathland is 5km off A169 Whitby/ Pickering road. From Goathland cross to the far side of the green to drop down via narrow lanes into Beck Hole (1km) with pub and bridge. From here footpath runs up Eller Beck's R bank for 600m to the falls, with the railway above. Mallyan Spout is 2km up West Beck, in opposite direction from Beck Hole, through Comb Wood. Pretty but no swim or plunge pool here (www.beckhole.info, www.nymr.co.uk).

123 Falling Foss

Town: Ruswarp
Grid ref: NZ 888035
Postcode: YO22 5JD (400m S)

Water quality: A
Depth/size: plunge, paddle

Walking: 45 mins, moderate
Train: Ruswarp, 6km
Extras: Whitby sands

ℹ️ A tall plume and small deep plunge pool (10m high, 2m deep) at the head of a forested gorge. Shingle beach. Overlooked by path but feels secluded. Difficult scramble down.

▶️ From Ruswarp station (near Whitby) follow B1416 (S, dir Scarborough) and take the 'middle' R after 4.8km. (Do not take hard R, to Littlebeck, or 'straight-on' R over cattle grid). Follow lane for 1.5km to car park. Continue down through woods on foot to find falls. To reach base walk downstream and descend into gorge, then follow stream bed back up. Also small pool upstream of Midge Hall (50m).

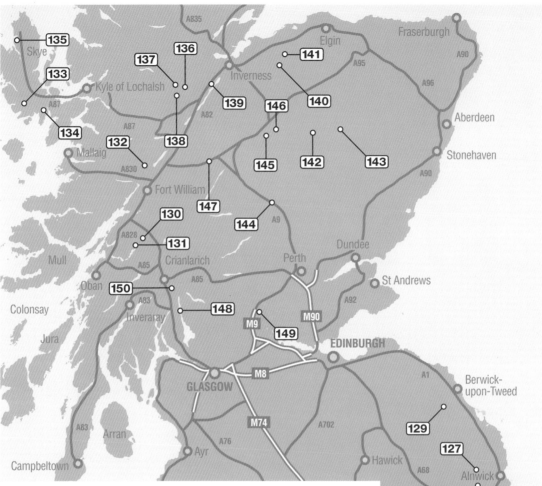

Highlights

125–126 Swim with the Romans along Hadrian's Wall and visit their temple to the water nymphs

127 The bottomless plunge pool of Linhope Spout in the grand Cheviot Hills

129 Swim across the border from England to Scotland at Union Bridge, one of the oldest suspension bridges in the world

130–131 The magical Glen Etive is the less-visited offshoot of Glen Coe, good for wild camping by its fantastic series of river pools

133–135 The Faeries and Faerie Pools of Skye, the clearest water in Britain

138 Scotland's second highest waterfall with a dramatic plunge pool too

139 Bathe with the Loch Ness Monster by the ruins of Urquhart Castle

146 Swim across to a ruined castle island on Loch an Eilein

148 Find Rob Roy's secret cave on the bonnie banks of Loch Lomond

149 The closest thing to Highland pools without going north of Stirling. There's an excellent pub nearby too

150 Swim in Rob Roy's giant bathtub at the Falls of Falloch

Scotland and North

This vast region takes us from Hadrian's Wall and Northumbria up into the great mountain massifs of Scotland. From Glen Coe to the Isle of Skye, Findhorn to the Royal Dee, Loch Ness to Loch Lomond, we explore the legend and history of Scotland's wild-swimming waters.

△ **126** North Tyne River downstream of Chesters Fort

North Pennines and Hadrian's Wall

Heading north from the Yorkshire Dales, along the spine of Lune Moor, great long trails of pink cloud were reaching into the sky. I camped by moonlight in a large meadow on the banks of the River Tees, close to Low Force, before continuing on to Hadrian's Wall. The plan was to find the shrine of the water goddess Coventina and swim in the same spots as the Romans at Chesters Fort and Broomlee.

The North Pennines traditionally marked the last frontiers of Roman Britain; a great march of barren hills and plunging dales growing more desolate as they reached the border with the Picts. For the southern Mediterranean Roman soldiers stationed here in the second and third centuries AD the wet climate must have been very different from their dry and dusty homeland. They brought with them an adoration for springs, running water and river gods, all of which were to be found aplenty in ancient Britain. At Brocolita Fort on Hadrian's Wall they built one of the best preserved 'nymphaeum' shrines in the country. The water temple consisted of three altars to the part-Celtic, part-Roman water goddess Coventina. The inscriptions show her reclining with flagons and palms, protecting the three springs with her nymph assistants.

The great wall was begun in 122AD and acted as a working defence for over two hundred years. Its remains run intermittently across the countryside, in some places a ragged ruin – much was taken to

△ 125

△ 125

△ **125** Roman water goddess Coventina

build the roads of Newcastle in the eighteenth century – but in more remote parts there are miles of surviving fortifications with milecastles and forts still standing among crags and tarns. In this central Pennine section the wall hugs a long dolerite escarpment, a natural defence, with lakes forming in the depressions below.

The Romans were very keen bathers and, though there was a bathhouse at Brocolita, it couldn't compare to that at Chesters Fort, three milecastles down on the River Tyne. With its endless supply of river water they were able to build a large bathing house complex. Its sixteen interconnecting chambers contained warm, hot and steam rooms and, of course, the cold plunge pools that are so central to Roman hydrotherapies.

There was once a great Roman bridge here and you can now paddle in the stream among the original bridge stones, scattered around like blocks from the Colosseum. Some years ago old Roman coins were found among the rocks and there are doubtless other treasures lurking in the riverbed.

The Romans were also excellent swimmers – it was a requirement of entry for the Roman soldier to be able to swim across a river in spate with full battle kit – but they would have had little challenge here. The river is mainly shallow in the vicinity of the ruined bridge, but there are deeper holes if you explore a little way downstream on the far bank.

The main Roman swimming was at Housesteads Fort, the most extensive and best preserved of Roman wall fortifications, and three milecastles to the west of Brocolita. Broomlee Lough is just 500 yards down from the fort, across the moor into no-man's land. Today the local farming families still gather here once a year for their summer swimming party in the overhanging eaves of Dove Crag. The tarn is large, mainly shallow and surprisingly tepid but at this crag end the water is deeper and the cliffs provide enough shelter from the wind for the mallard, tufted duck, golden eye and coots that make forays out from the reeds to paddle under the great Northumberland sky.

North Pennines and Hadrian's Wall

124 Low Force, Tees

Town: Middleton-in-Teesdale
Grid ref: NY 904279
Postcode: DL12 0XF (400m SW)

Water quality: A
Depth/size: swim, dive, current

Walking: 20 mins, moderate
Train: Appleby-in-Westmorland, 40km
Extras: High Force waterfall

ℹ This is the little-known sister of High Force. Still very large but with a deep, calm pool on a side channel by a wooded island.

◐ Middleton-in-Teesdale is between Darlington (A1M) and Penrith (M6) on B6277/A66. 1km beyond Newbiggin, 200m after telephone box, park in lay-by L. Low Force is directly below, but footpath is 400m on at Howgill House. Swim beneath minor fall on smaller side channel on near side of wooded island. Further 2km downstream there is huge sweep of riverside field and basic campsite: Low Way farm, Holwick (01833 640506).

125 Broomlee Lough

Town: Haltwhistle
Grid ref: NY 794697
Postcode: NE47 6NL (1km NW)

Water quality: A
Depth/size: swim, paddle

Walking: 30 mins, difficult
Train: Haydon Bridge, 8km
Extras: Housesteads Fort

ℹ Large open moorland tarn set beneath a crag and one of the great forts of Hadrian's Wall. Marshy, shallow shore in places but deeper in SE corner beneath Dove Crag.

◐ Housesteads Fort is well signposted along the B6318 wall-road (www.english-heritage.org.uk). From free car park follow main path up to fort (no need to pay unless you wish to go inside fort walls) and join Hadrian's Wall path on R side heading E. Continue 800m and, just after milecastle 36 at King's Wicket, bushwhack down over open-access land 300m to lakeside beneath Dove Crag. Brocolita is by road, 7km E.

126 Chesters, North Tyne

Town: Humshaugh
Grid ref: NY 914701
Postcode: NE46 4ET (300m SW)

Water quality: A
Depth/size: plunge, paddle

Walking: 15 mins, easy
Train: Hexham, 7km
Extras: Chesters Roman Fort

ℹ Shallow rapids among ruins of collapsed Roman Bridge. Chance to find Roman remains and examine Roman bathing complex. Deeper pools downstream.

◐ Chesters is 1km west of Chollerford roundabout on B6318. Entrance to site is £4.20 (www.english-heritage.org.uk). From shop cross site (400m) to bathhouse, river and bridge ruins. You are free to cross wooden fence and paddle in stream. The river is much deeper above Chollerford bridge (1km). A good footpath follows the North Tyne upstream 1km from weir on its L bank. Many deep sections (e.g. NY 929708).

△ **127** After a long walk to Harthope Spout, in the valley parallel to Linhope

Cheviots and the Tweed

To the north-east of Hadrian's Wall lie the Cheviot Hills and a Northumberland borderland contested for centuries by chieftains and smugglers. Deep remote valleys are rich in river pools and on the northern edge you can swim to Scotland across the River Tweed.

All is peaceful in the county now and much is protected in the fabulous and remote Northumberland National Park with Kielder Forest and the Cheviot hill range. Three river dales drain the Cheviots: the Harthope, the Breamish and the Coquet. The best-known pool on all of these is Linhope Spout on the Breamish, renowned for its unfathomable depth.

It's a long walk to the Spout but the high plume is worth it. It tips down a straight chute into an almost perfect cylindrical plunge pool on the edge of a wooded Breamish dale. Popular with walkers and families cooling off in the summer, there is a fun six-foot ledge from which you can jump. For the wildlife enthusiast, Linhope Burn attracts breeding birds like the dipper and grey wagtail – always on the move in their search for caddis-fly and other aquatic invertebrates. You may well also see an oystercatcher scurrying along the river bank.

The River Coquet is easier to reach, but feels just as remote. A winding mountain lane runs for many miles to the head of the dale. Here it meets the Scottish border and the remains of Chew Green Roman Fort, an old staging post on the road from York to Scotland.

△ 129

△ 127

△ 129

I followed the road to Linbriggs and Sillmoor and a stretch of perfect river pools bounded by grassy moor. The current was just strong enough to pick me up and propel me down the chute of the mini-waterfall. Although the river is generally shallow, it's possible to swim down for at least half a mile, mainly carried by the flow, with a few strokes here and there to keep up the momentum.

Harthope is in the emptiest of the Cheviot valleys with a long approach walk. It's in the valley north of Linhope and the Breamish. The plunge pool is magical, deep and cave-like with mosses climbing up the steep black grotto walls. Finding Harthope Spout, hidden in the crevice of a wooded hollow, is quite an achievement and it makes a wonderful place to skinny-dip.

The Harthope and Breamish rivers both join the Till, which flows north into the Tweed. This, in turn, forms the border with Scotland in its final 20 miles. The Union Bridge was the longest suspension bridge in the world when it opened in 1820 and finally linked the east coasts of England and Scotland. Oddly the Scottish end is actually south of the English side! It has long been famous for eloping couples keen to wed under more liberal Scottish law: marriage on the Scottish side is legal even without the the 'reading of the banns' for three Sundays prior to the ceremony.

Given all this border history it seemed a good place to attempt to swim across the frontier. A friend and I arrived late one August afternoon for the challenge, the meadow beneath the bridge awash in head-high crimson Balsam. Parting the flowers to find the riverbank we stepped down into the pebbly river shore and began to walk out into the alarmingly brisk current. The wide stream proved shallow enough to wade but after a little orientation – swimming breaststroke against the flow and practising landing ourselves on the bank – we began our migration attempt, striking out at an upstream angle to try to hit the opposite side square on, and checking from time to time that we could still feel the riverbed with our feet. The passage was remarkably easy and the feeling of running the stream invigorating – so much so that we swam between the two countries several times before finding somewhere to get a cup of tea.

Cheviot and the Tweed

127 Linhope Spout, Breamish

Town: Ingram
Grid ref: NT 959171
Postcode: NE66 4LZ (1km NW)

Water quality: A
Depth/size: dive, plunge, paddle

Walking: 45 mins, moderate
Train: Alnmouth, 30km
Extras: Alnwick Castle

ℹ A 'bottomless' plunge pot, about 5m wide and circular, beneath a tall spout in a pretty glade that is ideal for picnics. Paddling in shallows of beck.

▶ From Ingram (5km off A697), continue on through village (4km) to end of public road then 1km further by foot to Linhope hamlet, turning L behind houses and then immediately R, to follow steep track, with woods on R, for 1km onto open moor. Follow signs to spout down below on R. Harthope Lin is a deeply hidden plunge pool (NT 928202) 5km NW of the Spout, or 5km SW of Wooler, 3km from road end on the Harthope Burn.

128 Sillmoor, Coquet

Town: Alwinton
Grid ref: NT 891073
Postcode: NE65 7BN (1km SE)

Water quality: A
Depth/size: swim, plunge, current

Walking: 2 mins, easy
Train: Alnmouth, 35km
Extras: Chew Green Roman Fort

ℹ Open meadows and moorland along banks of delightful River Coquet. Some rapids and a fall, but mainly intermittent river pools about 2m deep.

▶ Between Jedburgh and Alnwick, follow the lane into the Cheviots 3km beyond hamlet of Alwinton to cross river Coquet at Linbriggs farm (gorge, rapids and pools below) and continue 1km to park by river. Picnic place and small pool but follow river downstream, up to 300m by round sheep pen, finding deeper river pools. Follow the road a further 13km up on the Cheviot ridge to find Scottish border and the Roman Fort of Chew Green.

129 Union Bridge, Tweed

Town: Horncliffe
Grid ref: NT 933514
Postcode: TD15 2XT (1km NW)

Water quality: A
Depth/size: swim, current

Walking: 20 mins, moderate
Train: Berwick-upon-Tweed, 10km
Extras: Norham Castle, 4km upstream

ℹ Wide (80m), shallow (1m), fast flowing stretch of Tweed, downstream of bridge. Fun to swim against current and cross to Scotland! Dangerous in high water.

▶ Horncliffe is 7km SW of Berwick-upon-Tweed. Follow signs to Union Bridge and follow river's R path downstream 200m, crossing L onto island. 85km upstream, in Scotland, the much smaller Tweed is idyllic in the broad meander beneath Neidpath Castle just outside Pebbles (NT236405, EH45 8NH). Two deep pools linked by shallow rapids are accessible from the river's L bank off A72 1.5km E of Pebbles.

△ **131** In the long river canyon, Lower Glen Etive

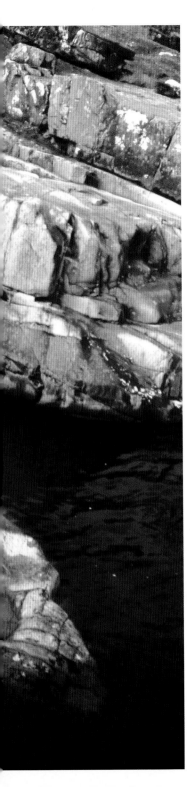

Glen Etive and Loch Arkaig

Glen Coe is famous for its wild and dramatic scenery but it is a little known valley running to the south that holds its most spectacular swimming pools and gorges. A haven for climbers and wild campers, Glen Etive is a place you could spend many days exploring.

Picking up a friend in Glasgow on her first visit to Scotland we drove north past Loch Lomond in the evening light before climbing up through the craggy lakes of Rannoch Moor as dusk fell. Arriving at King's House Inn at Glen Coe we pitched our tents in the darkness with the black outline of Aonach Eagach towering over us against the indigo sky. Apart from catching the occasional glint of foam flashing in our headlights, we could only hear the nearby river and could only hope we hadn't camped too close to its edge.

The whole valley was still in shadow when we awoke the next morning but the sun had caught the top of the mountain and was playing with wisps of cloud. Here, under the dark guardian of Buchaille Etive Mor – The Great Shepherd of Etive – we found ourselves by the most fantastic series of river pools you can imagine. A few yards away our grassy bank dropped into a gentle river lido in a wide meander with a shingle beach and a hundred yards downstream it tumbled into a long gorge with deep lagoons and purple-streaked cliffs.

It was to this beautiful glen that Deirdre, foremost heroine in Irish mythology, came to escape Conor Mac Nessa and his warriors.

△ **130** Beneath the high falls, Higher Glen Etive

△ **132** Middle Pool

△ **132** Fly Agaric

△ **130** Pebbles in stream

Her twisted yellow tresses and grey–green eyes were said to lure the gods and mesmerise the mortals. That morning, as the shadow line edged down the mountain wall and the sun broke the high peaks with blinding rays, there was something of her colours in the dawn sky.

The tiny road follows the river for over eight miles down to the remote and enchanted sea loch of Etive. The gorge by which we camped remains my favourite place but there are many other swimming holes as well. A mile upstream there are good shallows for children with a small island and further on the river plunges through a waterfall to open onto a long pool. Two miles before the road head of Glen Coe are deep plunge bowls scooped out of the blue stone, each a bathing place to while away a whole day.

Thirty miles to the north of Glen Coe, on the other side of Fort William, you'll find the Dark Mile, a long line of beech trees and a stone bridge across the Caig Burn. To the right the Eas Chia-aig Falls tumble into a deep, dark pool known as The Witch's Cauldron. An old woman was accused of casting her evil eye over Lochiel's cattle, causing them to fall ill and die. When she fell into the pool and drowned the cattle miraculously began to recover from their illness. There are three tiered pools and, while the lower is the largest, the upper two have wildly contorted rock striations that are particularly noteworthy.

There may have been some witch-like trickery going on the day we were there. Having dipped in The Witch's Cauldron we headed further up the remote lane to find somewhere to swim in Loch Arkaig. We quickly passed an unusually early crop of red and white toadstools on the roadside, the magic mushroom Fly Agaric. Suddenly a stone on the road cut open not one but two of the tyres on the car. We had no phone reception and were stranded by the loch overnight. This gave us plenty of time to explore the white shingle beaches and swim but we couldn't help but feel we had been tricked by The Witch's Cauldron and her toadstools.

Glen Etive and Loch Arkaig

130 Higher Glen Etive

Town: Glencoe
Grid ref: NN 224521
Postcode: PH49 4HY (4km SW)

Water quality: A
Depth/size: plunge, paddle

Walking: 2 mins, moderate
Train: Bridge of Orchy, 27km
Extras: Kings House Hotel

ℹ️ A dramatic glen with perfect river pools running very close to road. Good pub nearby in the grandeur of Glen Coe.

▶️ Glen Etive is a narrow road off the well-known A82 through Glen Coe S of Fort William. Coming from the SE, turn L 1km after the Kings House Hotel (www.kingy.com) then 3.5km further on look for plunge pools and waterfall on L. A further 2km on brings you to a much higher falls which is hidden 50m from the road. The river flows through a pretty canyon below it with some deep sections before rejoining the road after 100m.

131 Lower Glen Etive

Town: Glencoe
Grid ref: NN 180511
Postcode: PH49 4HY (6km SW)

Water quality: A
Depth/size: plunge, swim, paddle

Walking: 2 mins, moderate
Train: Bridge of Orchy, 29km
Extras: Red Squirrel campsite

ℹ️ A long river canyon with high cliffs and deep water. Popular for wild camping.

▶️ As for Higher Glen Etive but 6.5km from main road you will come to a turning on L with a bridge and gates (Alltchaorunn). From here follow road exactly 2.1km to kink in river by road with large river pool in bend and space to camp next to it. Just downstream the river flows into 150m long rocky canyon with fantastic swimming. Nearest real campsite is www.redsquirrelcampsite.com, 01855 811 256, 10km, Glen Coe.

132 The Witch's Cauldron

Town: Clunes
Grid ref: NN 176889
Postcode: PH34 4EH (1km N)

Water quality: A
Depth/size: plunge, swim

Walking: 1 min, easy
Train: Spean Bridge, 8km
Extras: Clan Cameron Museum

ℹ️ A series of three falls and three pools set in quick succession by roadside. Interesting rock formations.

▶️ Clunes is 18km NE of Fort William on the B8004 then B8005 through dark beech woods along Loch Lochy. 2km further on find car park and bridge, next to the falls of Eas Chia-aig. The first pool by the bridge is deepest and largest (50m). Subsequent pools are smaller but more beautiful and can be accessed by dropping down from footpath. There is a further falls 500m up footpath. Continue (10km) to swim from wild and remote white pebble beaches of Loch Arkaig (NN 004922).

△ **133** Faerie Pools under the Black Cuillins

The Faerie Pools of Skye

The Faerie Pools on the Isle of Skye are so clear you have to stare to see if they have water in them at all. They lie serenely in a sheltered glade of lilac rocks and rowan trees while the misty towers of the Black Cuillin kingdom rise menacingly above.

Skye attracts visitors from all over the world for its breathtaking scenery with some of the most inaccessible wilderness left in Britain today. Rising like great Gaudi spires above giant basalt cliffs, the Black Cuillin Mountains are the remnants of huge volcanoes made up of gabbro, an intensely hard, old, green igneous rock usually found under the ocean. Now ribbed by deep scars and ridges, the combination of millions of years of constant rain and the extraordinary geology, they contain some of the clearest and most colourful waterfalls in the UK, plunging down the mountains to the ocean.

High in the hills are several 'Faerie Pools', renowned in local folklore for their association with enchanted beings. The best known are on Allt Coir a Mhadaidh in Glen Brittle. I arrived in the evening just as the peaks above had cleared for the first time in days. A crimson light was glowing on An Diallaid peak and the waterpipe gully that runs from top to bottom gaped open like a liverish wound. A mile up from the road the first sunken glade appeared like a safe haven within the mountain. The waterfall, pool and stream were all banked with berries and ferns and sheltered from the wind.

△ **133**

△ **134**

△ **134** Underwater gabbro

The pools, some tinged with pinks and greens, are lined with smooth rock like the inside of a woodturner's bowl. Two are linked by an underwater arch and, with goggles on, I swam back and forth examining the faerie underworld. The rock face was encrusted with pieces of quartz and there was an almost phosphorescent emerald glow. Deep down on the pool floor ingots of rock shimmered on the sandy bed. I stayed in the water mesmerised for almost twenty minutes before realising how chilled I had become and made rapidly home in the dusk.

It's not difficult to understand how this scenery became so imbued with fairy myth. Skye legend tells of local chief MacLeod who fell in love with a Faerie princess. The King of the Faeries, Oberon, agreed to a marriage, but only on condition that after a year and a day the princess must return to her own people. The marriage took place, and a son was born but the princess had to return to the Land of Faeries. She abandoned her child at Faerie Bridge near Dunvegan but the infant's crying tormented her so that she returned periodically to comfort him, wrapping him in her shawl. The shawl can still be seen today at Dunvegan Castle, now the flag of the MacLeod clan.

If you're still searching for faeries, you will find further pools off the Glen Brittle road and more in the burns draining the Red Cuillins on the Torrin side. Don't forget to visit the Talisker Distillery nearby, where the whisky is made with faerie water, or the gorge just south of Sligachan, where there are yet more pools. Then, up at Uig, north of Dunvegan Castle, find Rha Falls, a large plunge pot, and a mile further into the hills, the famous Faerie Glen, a glacial curiosity potted with many small, conical-shaped hillocks overgrown with thick, green turf rising several metres in height. The landscape is littered with bleating sheep and occasional strange yellow mushrooms of unknown power or use. I found a tiny loch there with a small brook running through it and a circle of stones, shaped like a spiral. According to legend, girls who dance naked on the spiral will have their dearest wishes fulfilled but that day the circle lay bare.

The Faerie Pools of Skye

133 Faerie Pools, Glen Brittle

Town: Bualintur
Grid ref: NG 436257
Postcode: IV47 8TA (4.5km NE)

Water quality: A
Depth/size: plunge, dive

Walking: 30 mins, moderate
Train: Duirinish, 50km
Extras: Talisker Distillery

ⓘ Deep pools and waterfalls, tinged with pink and blue hues, set under the peaks of the Black Cuillins. Perfectly clear water and underwater arch to swim between pools.

▶ From Sligachan (A87) follow A863, then B8009 and turn L just before Carbost (Talisker) dir Glen Brittle. Continue 6km to find 'Fairy Pool' car park sign. Cross road and follow clear path up valley to L of stream to the 'Allt Coir a Mhadaidh' waterfalls. Similar pools on mountainside further down road at Allt a' Choire Ghreadaidh (NG 417230) and Coire na Banachdich (NG 419215).

134 Faerie Pools, Bla Bheinn

Town: Torrin
Grid ref: NG 548215
Postcode: IV49 9BA (2.6km W)

Water quality: A
Depth/size: plunge

Walking: 30 mins, moderate
Train: Duirinish, 25km
Extras: Sligachan Hotel

ⓘ Dramatic waterfall gorge and numerous pools on route up to Bla Bheinn. Stunning and wild backdrop. Beautiful clear water.

▶ From Broadford (A87) follow B8083. 3km beyond Torrin find car park and follow clear path up to R of stream to find main waterfall after 1km. If travelling via Sligachan Hotel (01478 650204) to the Faerie Pools you will find further swims on the Allt Duraich Burn (NG 492294). Cross old bridge and main river from hotel and bear R to find gorge of tributary. Follow stream to head of its ravine, 600m from road bridge.

135 Rha Burn and Faerie Glen

Town: Uig
Grid ref: NG 396643
Postcode: IV51 9XP (200m N)

Water quality: A
Depth/size: plunge

Walking: 30 mins, moderate
Train: Duirinish, 50km
Extras: Faerie Glen

ⓘ Small lake by roadside in the pointy-hilled Faerie Glen. Large waterfall plunge pool nearby.

▶ As you approach Uig the lane to Faerie Glen is on the R, opposite the tower and by the hotel. Continue for 2km to find a small loch on the R side of the road (NG 415631) and some of the best fairy mounds and basalt columns. Back to main road and into Uig, 1km further on take the Staffin road by the police station and 50m on, before bridge, find a stile on R. Follow path through deep glen with the magnificent double waterfall of the Rha Burn (NG 396643).

△ **136** Pool above Dog Falls, River Affric

Glen Affric, Dog, Plodda Falls

Glen Affric is a refuge for one of Scotland's largest remaining stands of rare, ancient Caledonian pine. You'll also find Scotland's second highest waterfall here and a loch with an archipelago of forest-clad islands.

Scots or 'Caledonian' pine once made up the great ancient forests of Scotland. This magnificent old tree is entirely different from the regimented rows of conifers you now see in forestry plantations. Baobab-like in its grace, statesmanlike in its size, its boughs make graceful open arcs and its bark is gnarled and red. No two are ever the same. The Affric woods properly start as you approach Dog Falls, where several old pines stand cantankerously by the riverside. Ten minutes downstream you'll come to plunge pools ideal for bathing with hot rocky shelves to lay out a towel and dip in a toe. Further below are the main falls, a narrow plummeting chute into a gorge. A footbridge crosses some way down and from here it is possible to swim in the deeper water and explore the cliffs on either side.

The lane winds further up into the glen. At a sudden brow there is a promontory peeping out through the trees and Loch Beinn a Mheadhoin opens up, covered by a scattering of closely interconnected forest islands. There is something about an island, a place of adventure yet retreat, which I've never been able to resist.

△ **137**

△ **136** Caledonian Scots Pine

△ **138**

The thought of island-hopping creates even more excitement. Examining the map we located a point on the shore where the straits narrowed to only a hundred yards. With our inflatable canoe it was possible for two people to swim safely across to this refuge, with wide beaches and watery vistas. From there we circumnavigated the nearest island in an afternoon – part swimming, walking and boating – then struck out to the second.

The road actually ends as Loch Affric begins. From here truly wild territory begins, reaching into the heart of the Highlands, where the forest has stood for over 8,000 years, since after the last ice age. Bonnie Prince Charlie hid here after the Battle of Culloden and many of the trees are over 500 years old. Roe, sika and red deer are all present. Watch for them at dawn or dusk on the open hills above the tree line. Pine marten have increased in numbers over the past ten years, although their nocturnal habits make a sighting unlikely. Red squirrel, otter, brown and blue hare may be found too. Keep an eye open for buzzard, golden eagle or dipper by the water's edge. You may even encounter a wildcat or adder.

After a day of island-hopping and dipping at Dog Falls we camped in deep forest near Plodda Falls in the parallel valley of Abhainn Deabhag. Here is one of the most spectacular falls in Scotland, yet we were alone as we descended through the forest of Douglas fir the next morning. From the old Victorian viewing platform, on the edge of a 150-metre high precipice, miles of woodland open out across a great tropical gorge. A treetop dawn chorus was in full swing and down below we could see a giant pool. The path to the bottom of the falls was slippery and difficult but the pool was still and calm, with wood sorrel on the banks and only a small stream flowing into it from way on high. Once upon a time many people must have visited this place – an old wrought-iron walkway is still visible around the edge – but we swam in the great gorge as if no one had been here for years with just a circling buzzard above and the birdsong through the trees.

Glen Affric, Dog, Plodda Falls

136 Dog Falls

Town: Cannich
Grid ref: NH 288283
Postcode: IV4 7NB (2.5km W)

Water quality: A
Depth/size: plunge, swim

Walking: 10–20 mins, moderate
Train: Beauly, 40km
Extras: Scots pine forest walks

ⓘ Beautiful stretch of river among woods of Scots pine. Good plunge pools above falls. Further down there's a deep canyon and you can swim up to the base of falls.

▶ From Cannich follow the Glen Affric road for 7km to find the forestry car park on L. Admire the Scots pines by the river here and follow path downstream 250m to find rapids and fun plunge pool. Continue on path, along road and back down to river to find lookout over main falls (200m). Continue further on 200m to footbridge and deep canyon through which you can swim up to the main falls.

137 Loch Beinn a Mheadhoin

Town: Cannich
Grid ref: NH 247265
Postcode: IV4 7NB (7.9km W)

Water quality: A
Depth/size: swim, dive

Walking: 1 min, moderate
Train: Beauly, 50km
Extras: Loch Affric

ⓘ Stunning islanded lake, rich in original Caledonian pine. Many places to swim from shore and potential to swim out to islands if you have boat support.

▶ From Cannich continue 7km, past Dog Falls car park and a further 4.9km looking out for track on sharp L turning down to lake shore. After 300m this leads to clearing and good private place to swim. 500m further on, and for those with boat support, there is car park/picnic spot and a narrow (100m) channel to one of the islands. Also there's a narrow crossing from the peninsula at NH 261269, back towards Dog Falls.

138 Plodda Falls

Town: Tomich
Grid ref: NH 277238
Postcode: IV4 7LY (3km SW)

Water quality: A
Depth/size: plunge, dive, swim

Walking: 30 mins, difficult
Train: Beauly, 50km
Extras: Tomich Hotel and pub

ⓘ Deep, large, black plunge pool (30m) at base of Scotland's second highest waterfall. Difficult scramble but stunning views in this deep forested canyon.

▶ Tomich is 7km SW of Cannich on minor road parallel to Glen Affric road. From Tomich (www.tomichhotel.co.uk) continue further 4.9km, eventually on forestry track, to small car park. Drop down through woods, first to roped-off view-bridge to admire panorama, then to base of falls via steep, slippery path. Continue scramble to main plunge pool below second (minor) fall. Remains of Victorian viewing gangways can be seen.

△ **139** Swimming back from Castle Urquhart on Loch Ness

Findhorn and Loch Ness

High above Loch Ness, in the Monadhliath Mountains, the enchanted River Findhorn gathers its waters and prepares to carve out a string of gorges and river pools inhabited by gods and satyrs.

As you leave Glen Affric it's impossible to avoid the Loch Ness Monster tourist bonanza centred on Drumnadrochit and it seemed a little churlish to miss the chance for a swim with Nessie. The ruins of Urquhart Castle seemed the most impressive place to dip but, determined to avoid the crowds and coaches, I walked up the road a way and dropped down through a steep field of yellow mullein and butterflies to reach a more peaceful section of the shoreline.

A lochside ruin can never fail to impress in Scotland. More than once during its troubled 700-year history Urquhart was able to hold out because it could be re-supplied by ship. As I swam a little way out into the castle's hidden bay I had a fish-eye view up to the battlements and could see at first hand the great rocky bluff on which it had been built.

If you really want to swim with Nessie, though, she'll undoubtedly prefer the many more peaceful bays on the far south side of the Loch. I decided to leave her alone and head on to explore the Findhorn, one of the longest rivers in Scotland and one that rises in the Monadhliath

△ **140** Rhino rock

△ **141** Muckle Spate flood stone

△ **141**

Mountains above Loch Ness. Famous for its mystical qualities and great legends it has associations with *Macbeth* at nearby Cawdor Castle (where King Duncan is said to have been murdered) and more recently the spiritual eco-village of Findhorn, where residents believe the river is sacred and marks a border between the earth and the spirit worlds.

At Randolph's Leap, a narrowing gorge overlooked by shelves of yew and Scots pine woodland, the black peaty Findhorn water twirls and swirls through fissures. It passes over large river stones carved and curved by flood eddies and opens onto a wide calm pool dotted with islands and bays. On the sunny afternoon I was there it did indeed seem like the place to meet Pan and his nymphs and to frolic and gambol with the satyrs.

As you wander around these woods look out for the two flood stones, protected in iron cages, which look a little like gravestones. They mark the upper reaches of the great Muckle Spate of 1829, probably the greatest British flood ever. After a sultry week in August a thunderstorm began over the Monadhliath Mountains. It rained for three days and three nights and all the bridges except nearby Dulsie were washed away. The position of the stones show how high the waters rose, climbing over 30 feet and consuming vast tracts of land on both sides of the valley.

The bridge at Dulsie only survived because the gorge that it spans is so high. Yet the spate came to within a foot of its central keystone. This is a well-known beauty spot. The path above the bridge leads down to rocky shallows. Below the bridge there is a large area of calm, deep water where a waterfall joins from the right bank beside a small sandy bay. Silver and downy birch shade the river banks, with rowan, willow and bird cherry, and there are great stands of aspen, now rare in Scotland. Dippers and osprey are also sometimes seen and, if you look carefully, there is a rock remarkably similar to a rhinoceros bathing in the pool below.

Findhorn and Loch Ness

139 Loch Ness

Town: Drumnadrochit
Grid ref: NH 530288
Postcode: IV63 6TU (2.5km SE)

Water quality: A
Depth/size: swim

Walking: 15 mins, moderate
Train: Inverness, 25km
Extras: Urquhart Castle

ⓘ Britain's longest lake and home to Nessie. Secluded place to access shoreline opposite dramatic Urquhart Castle, down through fields. Rocky shelving shoreline.

▷ Park at Urquhart visitor centre just S of Drumnadrochit and continue up road 300m on foot. As road bends to L find gate into field opposite and drop down hill and to R towards wooded shoreline. Access water from small beach opposite castle and its landing pontoon. There is also access to loch along whole length of A82 but the most secluded locations are on opposite shore, B852 from either Fort Augustus or Inverness.

140 Dulsie Bridge

Town: Dulsie
Grid ref: NH 933415
Postcode: IV12 5UR (350m N)

Water quality: A
Depth/size: swim, dive, paddle

Walking: 3 mins, moderate
Train: Nairn, 17km
Extras: Castle Cawdor

ⓘ Stunning gorge with rapids above and deep pools, waterfall and sandy cove below.

▷ Dulsie is 5km off A939 via B9007, S of Nairn. Park by bridge. Follow upstream path for view of gorge and paddling. Or climb downstream from bridge on river's L bank to access deep river pools opposite waterfall. Some submerged rocks downstream: take care. Just upstream of bridge (go under it) there is a very small sandy cove. Route via Cawdor Castle (8km form Nairn) to visit setting for Macbeth, www.cawdorcastle. com. Also close to Randolph's Leap.

141 Randolph's Leap

Town: Relugas
Grid ref: NJ 001499
Postcode: IV36 2QN (1km SW)

Water quality: A
Depth/size: swim, dive, paddle

Walking: 10 mins, moderate
Train: Forres, 12km
Extras: Logie Steading craft centre

ⓘ Stunning wooded gorge on mythical River Findhorn, descending to rocky headlands with access to river beaches and very large river pool (100m long, 2–3m deep) with islands. Some shallows for paddling.

▷ Relugas is 12km S of Forres via Logie (and its café and craft centre, www.logie. co.uk) on A940/B9007. On inside L of tight bend of B9007 find parking opposite gate and entrance to Randolph's Leap woods. Bear down to L to see the Leap, shallows and head of gorge. Bear down to R to find headland and large river junction pool with islands. Warm up with tea after at Logie.

△ **142** Linn of Dee beneath Victoria Bridge

The Royal Dee and Killiecrankie

The Royal Dee is a regal place to swim. You'll find Queen Victoria's bridge over the Linn of Dee, the stately Balmoral Castle and some extraordinary ice-age geology. Further west the Pass of Killiecrankie was one of Prince Albert's favourite places.

We don't know if the royal family like to wild-swim, but Royal Deeside is probably the best place to find out. The area has been the traditional summer holidaying ground for the royal family since Queen Victoria and Prince Albert bought the estate and built their gothic castle there in 1852.

There are some beautiful swimming stretches along the Dee. Downstream of Balmoral is the Cambus o' May – literally, the 'bend in the valley' – with a quaint white suspension bridge donated by a gentleman from Kent in 1905. There is a deep section here and the sandy banks and flat rocks are popular in the summer for picnics and swimming. The Deeside railway line used to run this way and the Cambus o' May station was regarded as one of the most picturesque in the Scotland, so much so that the directors of the Great North of Scotland Company had a special meeting wagon shunted out to it for their board meetings.

Just a mile up the valley is the Burn o Vat in the Muir of Dinnet nature reserve. Children love to paddle in this spooky cave and climb up the little waterfall above into the secret ravine. The glacial meltwaters that carved out this great vat 10,000 years ago were ferocious – the rounded sides and arched roof show that this was once a churning whirlpool. Stumbling upon this curiosity when the woods are empty is an eerie experience.

△ **142** Looking to Linn of Quoich

△ **143**

'We came to the Pass of Killiecrankie, which is quite magnificent; the road winds along it, and you look down a great height, all wooded on both sides, the Garry rolling below. I cannot describe how beautiful it is. Albert was in perfect ecstasies.'

Queen Victoria's journal, 1844.

Upstream of Balmoral and six miles west of Braemar – the home of the Royal Highland Games – you will find Victoria Bridge over the Linn of Dee, opened by Her Majesty in 1857, where the river passes through a furious and deep rocky gorge before slowing into shelving, sunny pools. From here you can also continue to the Linn of Quoich, a series of smaller waterfalls and rapids, popular with families. This is a fun but steep stretch of river with some plunge pools to dip in if you are cautious. If you look carefully at the river rocks you'll see the Earl of Mar's Punchbowl, a natural pothole, about a metre across, from which the Earl of Mar is reputed to have served hot whisky and honey punch to his Jacobite hunting colleagues in 1715. Three hundred years on, however, the bottom of the pothole has worn right through.

Referring to it as 'my paradise in the Highlands' it was to Deeside that Queen Victoria retreated when she was widowed. She suffered greatly after Albert's death and took refuge in her memories of their times together, of which their visit to the Pass of Killiecrankie, 25 miles to the south-west, was one of her favourites. Here, in a magnificent wooded gorge on the River Garry, a key battle of the Jacobite uprising was fought. The Soldier's Leap is the narrowest part of gorge across which some soldiers are thought to have leaped as they tried to flee in 1689.

Further below, hidden from the visitor centre and car park, is the river that Queen Victoria and Prince Albert looked out over so excitedly in 1844. On a midsummer day, a warm breeze moving the leaves, I swam out into the blue of a wide pool reaching the white shingle bank on the far side. There I lay, my eyes closed, feeling my skin tingle and dry in the morning sun. Otters, pine martens, red squirrels and flycatchers inhabit this gorge, but all I spied that day were flecks of white cloud floating on a jetstream high above.

The Royal Dee and Killiecrankie

142 Linn of Dee

Town: Braemar
Grid ref: NO 063897
Postcode: AB35 5YB (3km W)

Water quality: A
Depth/size: swim, paddle

Walking: 5 mins, moderate
Train: Dunkeld, 50km
Extras: Balmoral Castle

ℹ️ A dramatic gorge cutting down under an elegant Victorian bridge to deep pools and river beaches in open woodland.

▶ Follow the road opposite the church in Braemar W for 8km alongside the Dee (note several beachy swimming places below) to reach the bridge and car park. Walk downstream 100m, past the gorge, to find pool below. Continue along the road a further 6km to road end to find Linn of Quoich and many river pools upstream in woods (NO 116912). Take great care here as the current can be strong. Look out for the Earl of Mar's Punchbowl, a small round hole in the rock.

143 Cambus o' May

Town: Ballater
Grid ref: NO 420976
Postcode: AB35 5SE (100m S)

Water quality: A
Depth/size: swim, paddle, dive

Walking: 5 mins, easy
Train: Aberdeen, 50km
Extras: Burn o Vat, 3km

ℹ️ A gently shelving section of river beach, deepening to 4m, with large flat rocks on the nearside. Elegant white Victorian suspension footbridge. Pretty setting on a curving sweep of the Dee.

▶ Heading from Ballater on A93 (dir Aberdeen, turn L before the bridge), continue 6.5km and, 200m after the Cambus o May Hotel, find car park on R side of road. Follow old railway line footpath back up river 200m to find suspension bridge. Beach on far side. Also worth visiting strange caves in woods, Burn o Vat (NO 420997). Continue further 500m on road, turn L and 1.5km find car park.

144 Soldier's Leap

Town: Killiecrankie
Grid ref: NN 916626
Postcode: PH16 5LQ (200m SE)

Water quality: A
Depth/size: swim

Walking: 15 mins, difficult
Train: Pitlochry, 6km
Extras: Killiecrankie visitor centre

ℹ️ A beautiful wide gorge opening out to very large, still river pool (200m). Access is a scramble but peaceful and private once there. Railway line passes above L. White pebble beach on far side.

▶ From Pitlochry town head out for A9 N but take the old road (B8079), not the A9. After 4km you will come to National Trust for Scotland visitor centre and car park (www.nts.org.uk). Follow trails down to the Soldier's Leap, a narrow chasm below R, but drop down to the L, via an informal path through steep woodland, to reach flat rocks by large river pool, about 100m downstream.

△ **145** Rapids above Feshiebridge

Cairngorms and Strathmashie

The Cairngorms National Park is the wildest landscape in Britain. Containing four of Scotland's five highest mountains the range is a rocky massif encrusted with snow and ice for most of the year. As one of the coldest plateaus in Britain it harbours wildlife normally found in the Arctic.

On the lower, warmer levels this granite geology has produced beautiful rivers and lakes. At Feshiebridge the river flows through smoothed stratas of deep grey, layered with vanilla quartz and blueberry granite. There are narrow pools and rapids upstream and on a hot day the rocks act as solar heaters, absorbing the sun's rays and transmitting the heat to the water with their fins. Under the bridge the water falls in a tumbling helter-skelter that has cut deep circular eddies and a moonscape of fantastic shapes.

The pool beneath the bridge is large, clear and still. On the left bank stands a solitary Caledonian Scots pine, at least two hundred years old, its trunk furrowed, its long lichen-clad branches arching down to sip from the river. Its old roots provide perfect nooks and crannies in which to curl up and sleep among the soft litter of the pine needles. Opposite is a sandbank of pure white rounded pebbles, a delicious location to swim out to. As you dive through the water you are struck by how clear everything is. Because of the granite the Feshie is not peaty like other Highland streams. Instead the water casts a golden yellow glow onto the riverbed and you can snorkel in between the rock shapes gazing at millions of years of time.

△ 146

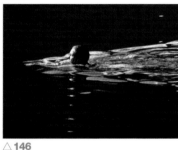

△ 146

△ 147

On the edge of the Rothiemurchus estate next door, the tree-lined Loch an Eilein also sits on the edge of the mountains, and at its centre is an island with a ruined, ivy-clad castle. Shrouded in the early morning mist this is the quintessential Scottish image. Estimated to be at least 600 years old, the castle fell into disuse several hundred years ago but its stones have lain protected by its island location ever since, though a small forest has grown up inside.

The swim across to the island is probably not encouraged by the estate, but is serene nonetheless. The loch waters lie still beneath the gently shelving banks and although the castle is only a hundred yards from the shore the backdrop of the Cairngorms beyond rises thousands of feet high.

Where the castle wall meets the water there's a small doorway through which you can clamber. Inside the old hall is complete with tumbledown fireplace and trees growing through the roof. Wildflowers have sprouted in the kitchen range and a family of crossbills have nested under an old stone seat in the small garden.

A further twenty miles along the Cairngorm ridge, following the valley of the Spey, the Pattack tributary offers more pools and swimming. Strathmashie community forest is justifiably popular with wild campers who don't want to stray too far from their cars. Within a few metres of the car park you arrive at a large amphitheatre-like bathing pool, idyllically situated among cliffs and waterfalls, with lots of space to swim and even a small beach.

In Scotland it is now legal to wild-camp an appropriate distance from buildings but this means the most accessible beauty spots are now littered with fire pits and loo paper. The Cairngorms may be the wild home to endangered species such as twinflower, capercaillie, dotterel and mountain hare, but it seemed unlikely I would find them at Strathmashie.

Cairngorms and Strathmashie

145 Feshiebridge

Town: Feshiebridge
Grid ref: NH 852044
Postcode: PH21 1NG (200m NW)

Water quality: A
Depth/size: swim, dive, current

Walking: 3 mins, moderate
Train: Aviemore, 12km
Extras: Aviemore

ⓘ Fabulous clear water flows down rapids into a large (100m) river pool (1–2m deep) with white shingle beach opposite. Interesting rock shapes and patterns. A large Scots Pine on riverside provides wonderful shade. A great fun location and one of the few with clear, non-peaty water.

▶ From Aviemore follow the instructions to Loch an Eilein but continue on B970 to Feshiebridge, parking close to bridge. Downstream, on L bank, you will find the tree and access to large river pool. Follow the forestry track up, past the house, 200m upstream, above the rapids, to find additional smaller pools.

146 Loch an Eilein

Town: Aviemore
Grid ref: NH 898079
Postcode: PH22 1QP (1.8km SE)

Water quality: A
Depth/size: swim, paddle

Walking: 15 mins, moderate
Train: Aviemore, 5km
Extras: Rothiemurchus visitor centre

ⓘ A small, romantic loch at the foot of the Cairngorms, with a tiny ruined castle on an island set 100m offshore.

▶ From Aviemore head S out of town (B9152, dir Kincraig) but turn L 1km after station on B970. After 1km, just before Rothiemurchus visitor centre turn R B970 (dir Feshiebridge). 1.5km turn L for Loch an Eilein and continue to road end and park (1km). Walk 700m along loch edge to reach castle. Swim discreetly. There are also many other places to swim on this loch (www.rothiemurchus.net).

147 Strathmashie

Town: Laggan
Grid ref: NN 566903
Postcode: PH20 1BY (1.8km NE)

Water quality: A
Depth/size: swim, paddle

Walking: 5 mins, moderate
Train: Dalwhinnie, 16km
Extras: Monadhliath Hotel

ⓘ A large calm pool beneath waterfalls on River Pattack in Strathmashie community forest next to car park. Pretty small beach area. Popular with wild campers and very near main road.

▶ 20km S of Aviemore leave A9 for A86 (Newtonmore) and continue to Laggan. 7.2km after Laggan look out for car parks L and R. Park L and find waterfall and pool below within 100m. Further narrow pools immediately upstream (200m) if these are busy. Or continue 1.5km to large waterfall, or another 1.5km to Falls of Pattack (NN 557883). Take care to avoid the informal toilet areas near some of the bushes.

△ **148** Loch Lomond at Inveruglas

Trossachs and Stirling

The national park of Loch Lomond and the Trossachs is home to several lochs and waterfalls imbued with Sir Walter Scott's legends and heroism, from Rob Roy's bathtub on the Falloch to the Lady of the Lake's island on Loch Katrine.

The Lady of the Lake has many incarnations in British folklore, but Scott's epic poem of 1810 is perhaps the best known. Set on Loch Katrine it features several young chief sons fighting for Ellen's love during the Jacobite uprisings a hundred years before. It's from Ellen's Isle (Eilean Molach) on Katrine that Malcolm Graeme, Ellen's true love, swims to shore in a fit of rage after his fight with Douglas.

There are several other islets nearby and it is quite possible, with boat support or in a group, to swim between them still. Access to these islands, and the entire loch, is only open to cyclists and walkers on a private, ten-mile road. The path does not quite loop around the whole shoreline but the cycleway does make a beautiful way to explore this remote and dramatic woodland with its countless places to swim and camp undisturbed.

Loch Lomond, to the west, was heavily associated with another of Scott's poems: 'Rob Roy'. Based on the real Rob Roy MacGregor,

△ **150**

△ **149** Sheriff Muir Inn

*'Then plunged he
in the flashing tide.*

*Bold o'er the flood
his head he bore,*

*And stoutly steered
him from the shore…*

*Fast as the cormorant
could skim.*

*The swimmer plied
each active limb;*

*Then landing in
the moonlight dell,*

*Loud shouted
of his weal to tell.'*

Malcolm Graeme swimming
from Ellen's Isle, in *Lady of the
Lak*e by Sir Walter Scott, 1810

the poem, published on hogmanay 1817, became so popular that a ship needed to be commissioned to take copies of the book from Leith to London, making Scott a rich man.

Rob Roy was painted as a colourful Scottish Robin Hood by Scott, though his adventures were heavily romanticised. He fought the upper classes, plundered cattle and joined the Jacobean rebellions with a dangerous band of 500 men. Many of Rob Roy's adventures were set on Loch Lomond, also made famous through Robert Burn's love ballad 'Auld Lang Syne'. This is the largest freshwater lake in Britain, set beneath the high peaks of Ben Lomond, and is dotted with islands to the south.

From Loch Katrine and the Trossachs a ten-mile, single-track road through unspoilt country brings you to Inversnaid, the location of Rob Roy's lochside hideaway. This cave can be found among great fallen rocks, its entrance quite obscured, only feet above the waterline. You can step out of the cave almost into the loch to swim. A few miles north, at the head of the loch on the river Falloch is Rob Roy's 'bathtub'. This is a stunning setting for swimming and picnics with a great shiny black rock vat set beneath the Falls of Falloch. Almost 100 feet across, with steep sides, it is one of the largest plunge pools in Britain and certainly makes an impressive place to take a bath.

In 1715 Rob Roy became heavily involved in the first Jacobean uprising. His men seized every boat on the Loch and assembled them at Inversnaid. He then set off to fight at the great battle of Sheriffmuir near Dunblane, 30 miles away, where the Earl of Mar was attempting to take Stirling. The battle was fought across the Wharry Burn, now a more peaceful series of small falls known as the Paradise Pools by the families who visit them from nearby Stirling. The shingle beach, plunge pools, rock slides and open meadows are set only a few miles from the motorway, making this an easy day out from Glasgow or Edinburgh. The famous Sheriffmuir Inn sits on the moor above and marks the site of the brutal and inconclusive battle. It was also once home to a famous wrestling bear. It now makes a pleasant *après*-swim location for a warming hot toddy.

Trossachs and Stirling

148 Loch Lomond and Katrine

Town: Inversnaid
Grid ref: NN 332100
Postcode: FK8 TU (2km NW)

Water quality: A
Depth/size: swim, dive

Walking: 30 mins, moderate
Train: Tarbet, 7km via ferry
Extras: Loch Katrine cycling

ⓘ Remote stretch of northern Loch Lomond on West Highland Way. Steep wooded rocky loch sides lead down to Rob Roy's Cave and the water.

▶ Inversnaid can be reached by ferry from Inveruglas (01877 386223) on A82 or via a long (24km) scenic drive from Aberfoyle. From Inversnaid follow Highland Way 1.2km to find cave signposted and marked with white letters on rock. It is only metres above the water line. For southern Loch Lomond try cove 6.8km N of Balmaha (NS 372957). Ellen's Isle on Loch Katrine is 10km N of Aberfoyle on A821, then 2km walk along the shore road (NN 491084).

149 Sheriff Muir Paradise Pools

Town: Dunblane
Grid ref: NN 819011
Postcode: FK15 0LN (700m SW)

Water quality: A
Depth/size: plunge

Walking: 15 mins, moderate
Train: Dunblane, 7km
Extras: Sheriffmuir Inn

ⓘ A perfect, if small, plunge pool in open countryside with a fun rock slide. Above are 100m of further little pools and cascades in woods.

▶ Close to Stirling and the motorways. Coming from S on M9 head into Dunblane (B8033) and at town centre roundabout (2km) take third exit on Glen Road. After 1.4km turn L signed Sheriff Muir (Sheriffmuir Inn, 01786 823285). After 5km turn R at Inn and after exactly 1.4km find gate (with 'No Litter' sign) on R. Walk down through fields 300m, under pylons, to find little wooded gorge with plunge pool and beach at bottom.

150 Rob Roy's Bathtub

Town: Inverarnan
Grid ref: NN 337208
Postcode: G83 7DZ (3km NE)

Water quality: A
Depth/size: swim, dive

Walking: 5 mins, moderate
Train: Crianlarich, 7km
Extras: Drover's Inn, Inverarnan

ⓘ A huge plunge pot under a great waterfall. The Falls of Falloch are spectacular and the great lido they have carved provides a large area in which to swim and dive. Further pools about 100m downstream.

▶ From Ardlui train station at N end of Loch Lomond continue exactly 6.7km on A82 to find car park and Falls of Falloch signed on R. From car park continue on foot 200m to find falls and large pool. Follow the woodland walk downstream Return 3.5km to Inverarnan for warming hot toddy at Drover's Inn (www.thedroversinn.co.uk, 01301 704234).

Games and Activities

To enjoy outdoor swimming in Britain it's important to be hot before you go in and to be able to warm up quickly after you come out, so why not have a few activities or games up your sleeve to keep everyone moving around?

A simple game of 'it' or 'tag' can be good with a small group but if there are more than four then some people will do less running than others. British Bulldog is better for getting the whole group moving. It's a traditional game in which everyone runs back and forth between bases, at least 20m apart, trying not to be caught by the 'bulldogs'. If you are caught you must join the bulldogs and help do the catching. The last person remaining wins.

To give this a watery feel play it in a shallow river with people having to wade or swim across. To spice it up a bit turn it into kiss chase: the bulldogs have to catch and kiss someone to make them 'it'. We call this Nymphs and Satyrs and its good for adults too!

Basic running races are fun and excellent for getting warm quickly. If there's no room for a full-blown race, then staggered time-trials, sending people off at five second intervals, are good. Why not make an interesting route with obstacles and activity stations – such as star-jumps and tree climbing – along the way? Three-legged and wheelbarrow races are fun and active as are cartwheeling championships and hopscotch relays.

Don't forget to bring a ball to play football, even if it's only two-a-side. A tennis ball or Frisbee can also make a very warming game of throw-and-catch, especially if your aim is very bad! If you are in a large pool then water polo, with ball or frisbee, will get everyone swimming wildly.

Ideas for other riverside activities

- Build river cairns or make rock arches

- Play Pooh sticks with your own boats made from reeds and twigs

- Use hazel twigs to dowse for some penny coins thrown into the grass

- See who can skim a stone with the most bounces

- Do some yoga in the water or on the bank

- Practise a synchronised swimming routine

- Learn to play the grass whistle

- Make a feather-and-leaf headdress

- Create the longest daisy chain

- Collect flowers and press them under a book using river rocks

- Find a four-leafed clover

- Paint yourself in mud

- Bring string and make a mobile out of branches and natural things you find

- Make a pebble maze

- Buy a disposable underwater camera to take watery photos

Water Fun

Mucking about in the water is one of the things that makes wild-swimming wild! Bring old plimsolls and goggles so you can explore properly: underwater there are fish, fossils and fantastic rock formations and there's lots of clambering around to be done along most rivers.

The ubiquitous blue rope swing can be found at almost every river swimming spot. It can be great fun plunging out of a tree and landing in the water, assuming it's deep enough and has no underwater obstructions. Several places are well known for their jumps, the Swims at a Glance section on pages 16–19 tells you some of the best. Start from a low place and work your way up as you gain confidence. Don't hang around at the top looking down and making yourself scared! And don't jump from more than five metres or you could hurt yourself.

In many places you'll find there's a current against which you can swim, like running on a treadmill. This is a good way to have a long swim in a small pool and it can be great fun trying to remain stationary without bobbing away. Where there are small rapids some people 'tube' down them on rubber rings or inner tubes, though Lilos are better at protecting your knees. This is quite popular on the Dart in Devon and the Wharfe in Yorkshire. Extreme versions of this sport are called 'hydrospeed' in France, 'river boarding' in the US and 'white-water sledging' in New Zealand. Take great care!

If you're not keen on swimming, a water fight is still fun. A supermarket plastic bag with holes in the bottom swirled around your head will send water spraying everywhere. Or buy everyone cheap water pistols and pretend you're in the Marines!